Pulpit In My Kitchen

A practical guide for wives, mothers, and grandmothers

Joni Campo

Dear & Precious Barbara, Your smile is a warmer — & you blessed us. Thank for a lovely day. Love, Joni

Published by
The Lighthousenet Publishing Company
Stuart, Florida

Pulpit in My Kitchen by Joni Campo
Published by The Lighthousenet Publishing Company
3275 S.E. Federal Highway
Stuart, Florida 34997, USA

www.pulpitinmykitchen.com

Scripture quotations marked (NIV) are taken from the HOLY BIBLE, NEW INTERNATIONAL VERSION®. NIV®. Copyright © 1973, 1978, 1984 by International Bible Society. Used by permission of Zondervan. All rights reserved.

Scripture quotations marked (NAS) or (NASU) are taken from the NEW AMERICAN STANDARD BIBLE® or its updated version. Copyright © 1960, 1962, 1963, 1968, 1971, 1972, 1973, 1975, 1977, 1995 by The Lockman Foundation. Used by permission.

Scripture quotations marked (NKJV) are taken from the HOLY BIBLE, NEW KING JAMES VERSION, Copyright © 1979, 1980, 1982 by Thomas Nelson, Inc. Used by permission.

Cover design by Terry and Judith Madden

Library of Congress Control Number: 2007904264
International Standard Book Number: 978-0-615-15111-3

Printed in the United States of America

DEDICATION

"You yourselves are our letter, written on our hearts, known and read by everybody. You show that you are a letter from Christ, the result of our ministry, written not with ink but with the Spirit of the living God, not on tablets of stone, but on tablets of human hearts." (II Corinthians 3:2–3, NIV)

To my husband Ted, my best friend, and the love of my life for over 45 years. His help and direction, as well as encouragement, to put these pages into print, have been my motivation. He has inspired me by his great faith and positive attitude: "I know you can do it. I'll help and God will do the rest!"

To our children. It is because of their presence in my life I have the privilege of being called "Mom!"

TJ, I love him most because he was first.

James, I love him most because he was second.

Stephanie, I love her most because she was third.

Claudia, I love her most because she was fourth.

Andrew I love him most because he was fifth.

To Missy, Kent, Amy, Jaime and Jason. I love you all because you are the highest and best spouses any mother could pray for. You love and challenge and complete my sons and daughters and I will always be grateful. The world may call you "in-laws", but, we call you "sons and daughter in love."

We dedicate this to our grandchildren; Hannah, Theo, Adam, Canaan, Madeline, Keaton, Grayson, Courtland, Reagan, Elena, Lincoln and all the babies yet to come but, eagerly awaited. Your presence in our lives reminds us over and over how much God loves us to have entrusted you to our family. We rejoice knowing that you are our continuity and God's way of assuring us that life goes on. You are our legacies to the world! We are indeed very wealthy people.

To our pastor, Tom Kehres and his beautiful wife, Becky, and our ever encouraging Church friends who have faithfully supported me in this endeavor. To our dear friends, Terry and Judy Madden, who not only created the wonderful book cover but, who have walked out relationships and parenting with us for over 25 years. Thank you! Thank you!

PREFACE

I have never written a book, but have long desired to. Finally, I believe it is time to pen all that has been placed in my mind and heart by a gracious and loving Lord. I feel commissioned to "start" and trust Him to lead my thoughts and ideas, my successes and my shortfalls. This may never be considered a "work of art" or a "great literary piece."However, I do believe that my experiences have not only qualified me to impart to others, but to bring some inspiration to just one lady, searching for her significance in what she may consider a dull and boring existence.

Over the years I have sat in many situations, business, social, church services and business meetings. There have been times when I envied the gifted musician, powerful woman preacher, Godly evangelist, the dynamic business woman. At one point in my life after we had sold our business, our children were all gone from home and my identity seemed nonexistent. I had been a stay-at-home mom, devoted wife, good daughter and fine sister. I lacked, in my mind, any major contribution to the world. I deeply wanted to "contribute". Several events woke me up to just how wonderfully meaningful my life was and is.

The first occurred when I read this: Franklin D. Roosevelt, in a speech during World War II said, "When all is said and done, it is the mother, who is a better citizen than the soldier who fights for his country. The successful mother, the one who is doing her part in rearing and training aright the boys and girls who are to be the men and women of the next generations, is of greater use to the country and occupies, if only she would realize it, a more important position than any man in it The mother is the one supreme asset of the national life. She is more important, by far, than any successful statesman, artist or scientist."

Secondly was a note inside a blank journal I had received from my son: "Dear Mom, We know you have lots of good thoughts and it would be a shame to lose them with the passing of time. As one writer put it, 'The faintest ink will outlast the strongest memory.' Happy Birthday, we love you a lot! TJ, Missy and Jones"

The third incident was a conversation with one our daughters. She reminded me that she was insulted when I said I had not made any contributions to impacting our world. "Mom, you hurt my feelings when you said that. You have five children and when we impact our world it has a lot to do with you."

I have mulled these events over the years. I came to a conclusion that there are many gifted women singers and musicians, great lady preachers, even great women in ministry with large followings. However, I and only I have the privilege and the right to minister to my husband and, though my congregation is small, it is to me the most important congregation in the world. My audience doesn't have a lot of glitter, but it surely brings a great deal of glory to the Father. My stage is not huge – maybe 10 x 12 or 20 x 40. It isn't surrounded by an intricate state-of-the-art sound system. The music in my house of worship isn't from a choir or worship team. My symphony comes to my ears from a crying baby, wrestling siblings, laughter and all the sounds of life that surround me in my temple. Accolades do not come in thunderous applause, but rather in the form of "Great supper, Honey" or "Can I have some more of that delicious great peanut butter and jelly, Mom?" And one of my favorites, "These are the best Frosted Flakes I've ever had!"

Finally, the reason for this book is to tell the world how much I have thoroughly enjoyed occupying the most magnificent pulpit in the world: "The Pulpit In My Kitchen!" I hope with all my being that the thanksgiving that is overflowing from my heart tells my Father in Heaven "Thank You, thank You, thank You!"

Contents

1 • MY MOTHER, MY MENTOR

Contrary to what most people think, mothers aren't born when babies are born. I came to that conclusion when the nurses at the hospital put my first bundle of joy into my arms. Like many new mothers, not all, I had anticipated an overwhelming sense of joy, excitement, and tremendous maternal feelings. Instead, I felt tired, uncomfortable and – quite frankly – very confused. I had expected an instant bonding with this tiny little creature. It didn't happen quite that way. I did the only thing I could think of doing. I counted his fingers, his toes and his ears. I still did not feel "motherly"! My only source of guidance and reference was my own Mom. Her advice was, "Time will change all of that!"

Over all my years of being a parent, my mother, Catherine Byrnes Burke, was my encyclopedia, my internet, my main reference. Born in Ireland, she came to this country by boat around 1920. Four years ago, my sisters and I, along with our husbands, and our daughter, fulfilled a lifelong dream and traveled to her hometown in Ireland, Castletown Conyers It was on that trip that I realized my mother was far more than "just a housekeeper and homemaker." She was a brave young woman who left home and came to the United States of America, solely on her own initiative Never had I visualized her as a pioneering, brave spirit. She came to an unknown place and took a job as an obscure cook on an estate on the North Shore of Long Island. As we stood in front of her home in Ireland, we had a very spiritual experience. We really experienced the bigness of God and how He moves the universe and all of us in it. My mother had tremendous faith in God and courage to leave this town – with four buildings, a church and cemetery – and cross a gigantic sea with little more than her few possessions, her younger brother and sister. Catherine learned mothering before she was a mother! Her legacy to us was her faith and her life of servanthood. She lived her life by "showing loving kindness to thousands, to those who love Me and keep My commandments," *(Deut.5:10 NAS)* It was the motto of her life. The Lord has indeed showered Catherine's children and grandchildren and even great-grandchildren with many blessings. She taught us by her life – not just her words. We often speak of lessons learned, sayings she used and stories she'd tell. The Irish have a great ability to embellish a story.

My mother married Patrick Burke, a chauffeur when she was 38. In four years they gave birth to three daughters and one son. Growing up, we had very little materially. My dad traded his chauffeur's cap for carpenter's tools. Living on Long Island we had long winters without work. Mom always made provision for long months without pay checks. We were not rich, but we were a very wealthy family. We had no television, but spent much time listening to stories of the "Old Sod". Sundays found us sitting on the floor while she read the comics to us. There were many times when she would comb our hair for hours. Winter mornings we awoke to the aroma of hot breakfasts. On Sundays there were always more people at our breakfast table with a feast of delicious food and fresh bakery breads. We learned the value of dinner time. It was always together – all 6 of us and then some. To this day I can remember when there were extra mouths to feed or when unexpected friends showed up, my mother suddenly being "too full to eat."

Each experience recounted had a lesson in it. We learned from Mom to care for our siblings, ("love one another as I have loved you"), share with any and every-one, *(Luke 6:30-31,* NIV) "Give to everyone who asks you, and if anyone takes what belongs to you, do not demand it back. Do to others as you would have them do to you."); to be hospitable "Share with God's people who are in need. Practice hospitality." *(Rom 12:13 NIV)*

My mother always cared for babies and the elderly. She never had any problem with color, size, accents or shape of the eye. *(Proverbs 20:10, NIV),* " Differing weights and differing measures – the LORD detests them both." *(Proverbs 20:23 NIV),* "The LORD detests differing weights, and dishonest scales do not please him."

When my sisters and I married, she embraced each of our husbands. The term "in- law" was rarely used. When our babies began to come into our lives, and her tents enlarged, she relished each new addition as if he or she was the only one. They – ten grandchildren – came into life with good parents, but the light of all their lives was "Grandma Burke." She always had time for them, played games with them, took them on long walks in the park. "Grandma B" played baseball cards with the boys and braided little girls' hair. There were times when she became such a strong defender of kid's rights that when we made them eat all their peas, or mow the lawn in the hot summer heat, we became her temporary enemy. Often times she would express a frustrated disapproval or come up with, "Aw, Ted, he's such a little guy," to keep them from getting chores to do.

None of us have ever looked at butterscotch candies the same in 45 years. Grandma always wore a dress with a pocket that held her stash of candy to treat them with. It was as if there was some secret between them, just the two of them, "that Mommy doesn't need to know." It was a treasure.

When our refrigerators would be covered with "stick figures", and we had little time to listen to the long tales attached to them, she had a way of never losing interest, or acting bored. Grandma would listen and listen. When we had an abundance of pictures we would mail them to Grandma so she could put them on her refrigerator. She sat through many boring concerts, dance recitals and athletic games. Every happening from losing a baby tooth to graduating from high school became a major event for her. When I would be ready to tear my hair out, or be desperate for some "peace and quiet", she would gently remind me that the time would come when my life would be so quiet and so peaceful, I would long for noise and activity. She was absolutely correct. Mom would also remind us when we were wishing for the children to be out of diapers, or in school, that "It's a sin to wish you life away. Enjoy it!"

I can recall expressing a concern when I was pregnant with our second child that "I'll never love this new baby like the one I have already." Her wise counsel, which I later shared with our daughters: "God will enlarge your heart." And He did, and He continues to enlarge our hearts as our family grows. "Enlarge the place of your tent, stretch your tent curtains wide, do not hold back; lengthen your cords, strengthen your stakes." *(Isaiah 54:2 NIV)* We all saw how she loved everyone the same, so we had faith it would happen for us too.

When our family moved to Florida, it was very difficult for both sets of grandparents. We were taking the great majority of the grandkids with us. She wasn't happy, but supported the move – at least to us. Larger events, confirmations, births and graduation now became occasions for a plane trip.

When TJ, our oldest son, was graduating from high school she flew in for it. She said to me "The Lord knows this may be the only graduation from high school I'll ever see at my age." And it was. The day after graduation she suffered a heart attack in Florida. While recovering, "Kitty B." met two native Irishmen at the hospital who were ministers and personal family friends of ours. I ran into them at the hospital and they visited her. Unlikely as could be, they had some in common friends from Ireland. When Paul and Nuala, the ministers, asked her "Do you know Jesus, Catherine?" she replied "Now, why wouldn't I? He's been so good to me, given me four children and ten grandchildren. Now why wouldn't I know Him?" Paul said, "Then would you follow me in this short prayer?" He prayed the sinner's prayer with her and all the angels sang ... "There will be more rejoicing in heaven over one sinner who repents than over ninety-nine righteous persons who do not need to repent." *(Luke 15:7, NIV)*

When I left my mom that day in the hospital, I called over to her bed, "I love you, Mom". She responded, "I know you do Jo. I know you do." When I returned to my office, I received the phone call. The doctor said, "We've had a tragedy here, Mrs. Campo." Catherine Byrnes Burke went home to be with the Lord. The doctor had no idea of the depth of the loss or the tragedy. She had a ripple effect on family and friends – it still goes on with our kids – although they are grown. She never played a big role in "THE Church", but rather walked the talk. Each of us has a treasure of fond memories, and a very rich heritage. We've inherited integrity, wisdom, servanthood, hospitality, kindness. We were most fortunate to have had her in our lives. She was a pioneer and an adventurer. I still, after many years, want to call and tell her, "We're having a new baby", or "Your grandson just got a new job," or I just want to call for a recipe, or get her advice on how to measure curtains or just visit with her on the phone, but I can't!

We will all sing the praises of our God for Kitty, my mentor, friend, ally, and teacher. During her lifetime people called her many names: Catherine, Burkie, Kitty B. Many called her friend. Only four of us and our husbands called her Mom. Her lessons are as lasting and encompassing as the skies. The lessons, like, "The heavens

3

declare the glory of God; the skies proclaim the work of his hands. Day after day they pour forth speech; night after night they display knowledge. There is no speech or language where their voice is not heard. Their voice goes out into all the earth, their words to the ends of the world." *(Ps. 19:1-4, NIV)* Mom's voice is no longer heard. However, day after day, her knowledge is poured out. She held our hands for a long time, but she holds our hearts forever.

Not until I became a mother did I realize how much my mother gave for me and my brother and sisters. Not until I became a mother did I realize that being one, lasted a lifetime. Not until I became a mother did I realize the work wasn't doing the wash, cooking, cleaning chauffeuring. It wasn't the work. It's being a different mother for each child; different wants, needs, personalities, temperaments. Not until I became a mother did I realize how much mothers overlook offenses and "underexpect" from her kids. My mother never consider our failures but, instead encourager us to try it again. Not until I became a mother did I realize how many disappointments my own mother had overlooked: birthdays that were forgotten, holidays when I was too busy to think of her home alone. Not until I became a mother have I realized none of that matters. What matters is having a higher regard for your child than yourself. What matters is the joy of having your child say, "You're my best friend!" or "Have I told you how much I love you?" or "When was the last time I told you, Mom, I really think you're beautiful?"

Never, before I became a mom, did I realize the small amount of faith I had. Being a mom is the ultimate walk of faith…faith to trust God for my lack of knowledge, understanding, faith for God to cover my failures and oversights, and for my not listening, for my lack of protecting my children. Faith to let them go to school, have friends, go away to camp, college, foreign countries. Only God can truly provide for them – using me, showing me, teaching me, and redeeming me. When I am not there, only God can be 24/7. He is the ultimate mother!

Of all the gifts my mother planted in my life, one of the most valuable is the attitude of gratitude and thankfulness. I never really expressed that to her. However, I must now say that her thankfulness for the fullness of her life was nothing short of spiritual. She always encouraged us in that. When I would complain that my car or washing machine was broken, she would remind me to thank God I even had one! When I complained about my noisy kids, or cranky husband she'd remind me to be grateful I had them in my life. She would awaken in me the need to live and breathe thankfulness and I would be refreshed and God would be blessed. Giving thanks is a beautiful gift to the one who is the recipient of the gratitude.

Take some time, alone with God, and reflect on your mother, mentor and friend. Meditate on all the blessings she's been in your life. Your very existence on planet earth comes from the availability of your mother to the very plan of God. Anything you want to say? Make it warm and let it breathe life into someone important in your life. She'll love to have you say it. If you can't say it, write it; then she can read it over and over.

Some of us found mentors outside our homes. Some of us had "mothers" who never gave birth to us. They were, however, mothers in real life, spiritual mothers, someone who spoke into your life and was there for you…a caretaker. Whenever one of our children was away from home, at school or a job, I always prayed that God would put someone into their lives to fill that gap of a "Mom." Those women visited my "kids" when they were sick, or in an accident, or even helped them pick out a suit for a big job interview. In turn I would try to be an encourager for a young person where I lived whose mom was elsewhere. Adoptive mothers, foster mothers, teachers, aunts (and even uncles) can all fill a gap. Stressed out and tired college students are often mentored and loved when they need a place to crash off campus. Sometimes their needs are filled by a caretaker who shows them the bed, let's them sleep round the clock and then does a carload of dirty laundry. I know of a mother (and father) who traveled "…halfway around the world to bring home a sister for their daughter" and another child into their home. I believe God has put "rescuers" in all our lives for a time when we most need them. These people are *MENTORS*. How sweet it would be to tell them, "Thank you."

2 • AFTER THE WEDDING COMES LIFE

Today's weddings are often a long time in the making. Everything depends on the budget, tastes and desires of the bride and groom – and often, the family. Every little detail is well planned and laid out. Caterers are interviewed, as are florists and photographers, dresses, seating arrangements, and on and on. Everyone will readily admit that no matter how long the engagement, how extensive the plans, the day is over before you know it even began. Brides are often heard remarking after the honeymoon, while looking at wedding pictures, "Oh, I didn't even see Sally or Joe," or "Wow, where did the day go?"

While all the plans are fun, even in the midst of stress, the wedding day is just the beginning of life together. Life takes working out and working on, whether you are a Christian or not. Marriage is still a life long journey. However, as a Christian, serving God first, I do believe the successful journey will become challenging and fulfilling. If being married means having all one's needs, wants, and desires met by another human being, then expectations can become frustrating and disillusioning. Only God Himself can fill all my wants, needs and desires! I can only satisfy my spouse when I serve him or her out of honoring and serving God.

There are many successful ministers of the gospel – both men and women. There are many successful singers, teachers, preachers, evangelists. There are, in my home church, all of these people. However, there is one ministry that only I can fulfill. Only one ministry that is my right and privilege to fill – that of WIFE AND LOVER TO MY HUSBAND! I may never speak in front of a large congregation or have a large TV audience, but I have no doubt in my mind or my heart that if I want to win someone to the Lord, want to demonstrate the love and grace of God, I must do it at home first. My most impressionable and valued congregants are the ones in my home. You may never have thought of your kitchen stove as a pulpit. You may not have ever thought of your bedroom or living room as a pulpit. Let me assure you that husbands, sons and daughters will learn more about the love and grace of God by the way you preach it in your home, by the way you love and serve your "forever" students.

Let's begin by talking about the husband and wife relationship. Oftentimes it is, and has been, easier for me to be a Mom than a wife, possibly because I was never commanded to become "*one flesh*" with my kids! Being a wife is the most challenging "career" I have ever had! It is also the best and least private career I have ever had. The day after our wedding, I didn't just awake to the realization my life was a "happily ever after" thing. Instead, it was an "Oh, my God, what happened to my Prince Charming?" This man was a man!

God took five days to create the earth and everything in creation. At the end of the fifth day the Bible proclaims, "And God saw that it was good." *(Gen. 1:21, NKJV)* and again in verse 25.

On the sixth day God said, "And God said; Let us make man in our image, after our likeness: and let them have dominion over the fish of the sea, and over the fowl of the air, and over the cattle, and over all the earth, and over every creeping thing that creepeth upon the earth. So God created man in his own image, in the image of God created he him; male and female created he them." *(Gen.1:26–27,* KJV*)*.

All the creatures on the earth were even named by the man. But, for the man there was no companion. After all God had created, He said, "It is good!" He had created man and then for the first time, God lamented; "And the LORD God said, It is not good that the man should be alone; I will make him an help meet for him." *(Gen.2:18,* KJV*)*

God recognized the first, not-right-thing in His creation. Aloneness. When both my dad and my father-in-law passed away, we saw the meaning of aloneness. Both my mother and mother-in law had families who loved them, but their lifelong companion was no longer there. (See section on *When Pulpits Change.*) When we visit our aunt in a nursing home, we grieve for her loneliness. She has very devoted family, but the real love of her life, her husband has been dead for over twenty years and she misses him more than her devoted family. I see people in restaurants eating alone. We all have single people in our families and churches who are alone. Some, not all, are happy that way. Most are just simply lonely. I see and talk to older people at my gym. When I ask them how they are, they make some kind of remark like, "I'm alone, and so, I come here to be with people." They expend more time exercising their vocal cords than exercising on the equipment! Several friends, after losing a spouse, have returned to work, not because they need the money but, as one friend put it, "I do it for my mental health." God recognized there was a problem in paradise. How much fun is paradise for me when I only have the birds, trees and animals to share it with? I want my man, my best friend, to share it with!

"I will make him an help meet for him. And out of the ground the LORD God formed every beast of the field and every fowl of the air; and brought them unto Adam to see what he would call them: and whatsoever Adam called every living creature, that was the name thereof. And Adam gave names to all cattle, and to the fowl of the air, and to every beast of the field; but for Adam there was not found a help meet for him. And the LORD God caused a deep sleep to fall upon Adam and he slept: and he took one of his ribs, and closed up the flesh instead thereof; And the rib, which the LORD God had taken from man, made he a woman, and brought her unto the man. And Adam said, This is now bone of my bones, and flesh of my flesh: she shall be called Woman, because she was taken out of Man. Therefore a man shall leave his father and mother and cleave unto his wife: and they shall be one flesh. And they were both naked, the man and his wife, and were not ashamed." *(Gen. 2:18-25,* KJV*)*.

ALONENESS

God saw the problem; God solved the problem. However, as much as we, as women (and men) do not want be alone, there are times when we desire to be selective and choose not being with our spouse, mentally, physically, emotionally and spiritually.

I want to be alone when I shop! My husband is a nightmare in a shopping mall! Shopping, for me, is an "experience"! I can look forever and enjoy everything I see, and buy nothing. That doesn't mean it was an unsuccessful trip. It just means I didn't buy anything. Ted, on the other hand, has an "outline" he follows when we go to a mall. "What are we going for?" "Where in the store is it?" "What entrance gets us closest to the section you want to go to?" "Did you have a specific color for the dress you're looking for?" Shopping, for my husband, is a hunting expedition. Find your weapon of choice, aim, fire, and get out!

There can be good times alone – alone with the Lord or sitting in a hot bathtub. I like sitting alone reading, praying or watching a frightening Florida thunderstorm. But the aloneness I am referring to is a separation of husband and wife spiritually or emotionally. We have ways of "shutting each other out" when we lose control, can't be bothered or are preoccupied in our own little world. Relationships take time, effort and energy. They require a dying unto self and death is not a prospect to be relished. If I have had a difficult day at work or with the kids, I can go into "silent mode" or cold-war mode. I can hide in my own thoughts and sulk so I don't have to share my heart with my spouse. Sometimes, I may even voice, "Just let me alone!" Other times, I can choose to even get in the Bible and "be with God!" When I willfully shut my spouse out even to do a "good thing," I am separating myself, not only from him, but I am perverting the best of things…being angry or separated from my spouse means s separation from God. I cannot work toward a better relationship with God, if I choose to be ignoring my husband. If I am NOT working toward being one flesh, I am working against it.

Aloneness is NOT a good thing. For some it may be a case of living with a spouse who is not a communicator. Men sometimes prefer being alone. However, how does that affect the bride? Psalm 102:6, 7: *"I am like an owl of the wilderness, like a little owl of the waste places; I lie awake, I am like a lonely bird on a housetop."* What to do! I have some lady friends who are married and experience loneliness in their own home. Some of the husbands want nothing to do with God or church. Their walk is not an easy walk, but they surround themselves with strong believing Christian friends; they reach out to others, like the sick, and minister to them. They are in a battle, but they choose to go to a weekly church bible study or church services. One friend says she, "just stands firm." I will not say it's easy to minister in your kitchen pulpit under these circumstances, but God is faithful. Be ready to be there for your husband. Don't put him in competition with God. Only God can fill the loneliness gap!

9

Aloneness is a choice. I choose to be in relationship or not to be. It is not good for man to be alone! It is not good for woman to be alone! "Alone" can mean being in the same room or house, or bed, and still be isolated and removed from each other. Being buried in front of the TV, reading, cooking or making the kids your sole priority, can all be ways of choosing to be alone from your spouse. Satan will even pervert motherhood, if we choose to be more in relationship with our kids, continually placing their needs and wants first, aside from our husband's. Children know how to be in control. Always remember, there will be a time when they will be living their own lives and separate from you both. Will you have enough left between you, to enjoy being just the two of you? When I make my husband my best friend, I have no fear of the "empty nest syndrome."

SUITABLE HELPMATE

"I will make him a helper suitable for him." *(Genesis 2:18, NASU)* Suitable, in Webster's dictionary is defined as "appropriate to a given purpose". Also, "to be acceptable or to fulfill a requirement, to follow suit or to fit in." A side note says, "suit the product or person to your specifications." None of the definitions or explanations mean "to be a duplicate of, or exactly the same as." Many times in the course of our marriage one of us would say something like, "If only we were more alike, we wouldn't have so many difficulties or disagreements." The truth is if we were completely alike, one of us would be a waste, one of us wouldn't be necessary! We'd be unsuccessful as a team and as well as boring and dull. If we were two exactly the same, we would be like a stutter! Repetitious! God in His wisdom has given each of us anointings, gifts, talents, and strengths to complete one another and become whole. It was, and is, His plan for us to complement and supplement one another.

Where my husband is aggressive, goal-oriented, and competitive, I respond so differently. I have a great idea, but often don't finish the plan. Where I am a "softy" and fall for every sob story going, he says, "Let's look at this a little more." One day in our real estate office a young man came in and offered me a card that said, "I am deaf, and cannot speak, would you help me out with some money." I was impressed with his clean cut look and went to get a check for him. Ted asked why. I told him. He said, "I don't think so. Who is he?" I didn't know since he came in off the street. Angry at my "tightwad" husband, I simply said to the young man (with a head shake), "No thank you". A short while later at lunch in a local restaurant, guess who was having an animated conversation with the waitress? I sometimes hate, HATE, that our differences keep me from making mistakes! What one partner isn't, thankfully, the other one is! Our differences are what make becoming *one* possible. We complement one another. We supply the missing ingredients in each other's weak areas and supplement each other by filling in the blanks.

3 • BECOMING ONE

LEAVING

"Therefore shall a man leave his father and his mother, and shall cleave unto his wife: and they shall be one flesh. And they were both naked, the man and his wife, and were not ashamed." *(Gen. 2:24,25, NKJV)*

When I met my future husband, we were in high school. After we decided to marry, I had no real problem "leaving" my parents' home. Love took away fear of moving out. Most young people look forward to leaving. It's the cleaving and becoming one flesh that demands the "working out."

The "leaving" must be done emotionally as well as physically. I cannot choose to be married to my spouse and continually compare him to the way my dad did this or that. It doesn't make my husband feel like the head of the home if I run to Dad for advice or have Dad come over and fix my car or dishwasher or paint my house. It might make Dad feel good and needed and wanted, but it can make my husband feel inferior, or not as competent as Dad. That's not leaving! It can cause my husband to feel like he's competing with my Dad. Some fathers still want to be the most important man in their daughters' lives.

We did a marriage seminar one year in a church that had a large number of families who were all interrelated. Everyone was somebody's cousin or aunt or uncle. Many of them were Italian. (I love Italians, I married one... very family oriented!). To summarize, several parents and their married children were all on this weekend. We were ministering about leaving your parents and cleaving to your spouse. At the end of the weekend, during a time of sharing, one younger wife said to her dad, "Dad, I have always called you over to fix all my problems because Charlie was always so busy making a living. I realized this weekend, Dad, that I have had you on the throne of my home, instead of my husband. Love you, Daddy, but, Charlie needs to be on the throne of my home." She had unwittingly put Charlie in competition for her affections with her father. She got things done around the house, but Charlie perceived his father-in-law to be the head of his family.

CLEAVING

Webster defines cleave in these ways, 1) to cling or adhere, 2) to be faithful. One of our friends in a married couples class described the meaning of the word "cleave" in terms he really said made sense to him. He worked for a large airplane manufacturer and recounted when he was working on putting parts together, the surfaces had to be extremely smooth, absent of dust particles or the smallest wood shaving of any kind. IF the smallest particle was tolerated, the two pieces would snap apart under pressure. Who wants to be on an aircraft that has the potential to snap under pressure? Marriage is the same way. It can snap under pressure. Therefore, we must endeavor to eliminate any *minute particles* that keep us from cleaving one to the other.

Living in your parents' home is from the past. When I got married, I was, and am still, a member of my parents' family; I just cleave somewhere else! It can no longer be whatever Mom or Dad want, but first what my husband wants and needs. The Bible tells me to "Honor my father and mother", but it also tells me, "For this reason a man shall leave his father and his mother, and be joined to his wife; and they shall become one flesh." *(Gen.2:24, NASU)* The reason we "leave" is marriage. The way we stay married is "cleave" – be joined to each other.

WHAT'S NEXT?

How do two people become one? Physically is easily understood. What about emotionally? I am who I am and Ted is who he is. However, one of the most challenging steps in becoming one is accepting one another for who we are. I'd love to change my husband. Most women overlook things when they're dating, with the idea, "I'll change that, after we say I do!" In our romantic minds, we convince ourselves that certain things aren't that important, now. Later, we'll see differently.

Some of the most endearing qualities and things that attracted me to my beloved, while we were dating, became the things that drove me and irritated me to frustration afterwards. I always liked the idea that he was a big guy 6'3". However, later I felt "squished" at restaurants and particularly when it came time to share a portion of the bed. I liked the idea that "big" meant he'd always be there to protect me. Then I encountered my first garden snake in terror, and he nonchalantly responded, "The snake is more afraid of you than you are of him." So much for being my big hero!

One of his most admirable qualities is his decisiveness. Then I recognized he was, to me, a control freak and a "must-be-in-control" person. I always respected the idea that when he saw something he wanted, he'd pursue it passionately. I resent being pushed. I think, think, think, and then I do! He thinks and quickly does. He takes chances, but I reason things through first. I'm cautious. I might want to pray about it first and then do it. What I used to admire as a strength, I began to see as "This man thinks he's always right." More often than not, he was right…a perfect choleric personality (a leader, a take-charge person, a risk taker)!

I was attracted to the fact that he was a "party" person. Loud. Got people going and moving. I'm not a loud person. I may talk a lot, but I do not elevate my voice. I hated "loud" (still do). But he can motivate people far beyond what they think they can accomplish. When he would come home from work, it sounded like he yelled "Hello!" I thought something was wrong or that he had run over a bike in the driveway. That's just him…his personality.

MAJORING ON THE MINOR

Most of the "intense" discussions (disagreements) we have are over little things. When we have major difficulties in our lives—relocation, losing an account, an injured child, cancer, or even deaths, we usually come together in strength. We bind together and fight the "big" problems as a team. However, we have the silliest discussions over the smallest of things. We sometimes MAJOR ON THE MINOR! We are different!

The first difference is Ted's a man and I'm a woman. Then add to the mix he's Italian and I'm Irish. Meatballs and corned beef!

My husband loves the heat, loves to sweat. When we moved to Florida from New York, I was half baked just contemplating the climate change. He dislikes air conditioning and paddle fans. I thrive on both! When we go to bed at night, I open the windows and throw the fan switch. Ted follows after me and lowers the window and shuts the fan! I love hot and spicy food with lots of garlic. My Italian husband didn't like any of that. Can you imagine an Italian who doesn't do garlic or "spicy"? That's changed.

I'm like a white tornado because I'm so disorganized. My husband, on the other hand, can tell if I've sat at his desk and moved a single item. He's very orderly and organized. I like to be early for appointments and my beloved thinks if you're early and need to wait, you're wasting time. One of our greatest areas for discussion is the way one of us drives and the other one, moans, sighs or back seat drives! Some of our most explosive moments are in our family automobile.

Get the picture? I'm sure you can relate. However, the whole point is that we balance each other. We supplement each other, complement each another. The places where we have differences need not be occasions for major disagreements. But, we do often MAJOR ON THE MINOR! We have agreement in the major areas: faith, finances, raising children, moral issues, and values. It's working on the small areas that seems to take the most energy and often is the cause of intense discussions. Recognizing that we are different and that it's okay to be different, has been a major victory for us. God created us as unique gifts to each other. Basically, our differences work for us, not against us. Accepting one another and letting God direct the changes makes it possible for two to become one flesh. Only God can perform this miracle.

NAKED AND UNASHAMED – INTIMACY

Here again, the "naked and unashamed" is more than physical. It's being open to share your innermost feelings, thoughts, and desires with another human being. Too often, I've heard women talk about their feelings with a girlfriend, but never with their husbands. Some of us "keep it to myself." It's an aloneness, a privacy. Most privacy is selfishness in disguise. Why am I afraid to tell you who I am?

When Satan tempted Eve in the garden, she decided she didn't trust God, so she took things into her own hands. Basically, Eve made a decision to go it ALONE. She didn't consult Adam; she didn't consult God. Eve wanted to do it alone. Adam and the future world have lived with that wrong decision. She wanted to be as God. Wives do not trust their husbands for varied reasons. A woman may already KNOW what her husband's counsel will be and doesn't really want to submit to his way. There have been times when I do not ask Ted for his opinion because I know very well what his response will be. Maybe a woman was betrayed by a father, a brother, an uncle… a man. So she isolates her feelings, or reacts to certain things because of past hurts. She chooses to be "alone", rather than become vulnerable. If someone she greatly trusted had earlier betrayed her in any way, she may have difficulty trusting her beloved spouse.

I've heard of a woman who got upset because her spouse came up to her at the kitchen sink and kissed her on the neck. She reacted with a startled response! Why? Because as a young girl, a male relative did the same thing and later on molested her. Her husband couldn't understand her violent reaction to a kiss. She never shared the incident with him. So, now we have two people who are confounded as to where this "emotional echo" emanates. Talk and share. Learn to be a student of your spouse and allow him to know you, intimately know you.

When Adam was fearful in the garden the scripture says, "they hid from God" because they were afraid. Women, do not hide who you are from your husband because you are afraid. Fear is from the pit of hell and is the exact opposite of faith. Without faith it is impossible to please God. Without faith in my husband, I believe it is impossible to become one flesh. Being open and honest with one another is the very beginning of intimacy.

When we dated, we shared everything. We didn't have a great deal of money, so we found ways to enjoy time together. We would drive to beaches, parks, and small interesting towns. One of our favorite pastimes was picnicking. I learned early on, that the best way to a man's heart is through his stomach! We spent lots of time together, talking about everything and nothing. We'd say goodnight after a date, and be on the phone shortly after! It's the way we learned about one another, our hopes and dreams. We became students of each other. Our "intimacy" was built on knowing one another and spending time together. It's the same with our relationship with God. For many years I was a devout churchgoer. I knew all about God, but I didn't have a personal relationship with Him. There was no intimacy with my Lord. I can tell you volumes about Mother Teresa or Laura Bush, but I only know about them. I do not KNOW them. I do not have a personal relationship with them. Relationships are built in time with the other person. How many of us enjoyed spending quality time doing nothing together and getting to know one another before we were married? After the wedding comes the marriage! We need to keep our priorities in order.

Intimacy in the bedroom begins early in the morning. Foreplay can mean taking out the trash, or bringing home some milk, or being on time for dinner, or calling each other during the day. Intimacy can be having a dinner for two at home, without interruptions. Intimacy longs to know how YOUR day went. When we had two children, 18 months apart, I was fortunate enough to be a stay-at-home mom. However, at the end of the day, I was so eager to communicate with someone who wore long pants, that I nearly attacked Ted when he came through the door. He needed a minute to be happy to be home, but I charged on relentlessly about how MY day went. Sure, I'd always say, "How was your day, Honey?" but if he didn't respond immediately, I would launch into my tale of woe about my day, he'd hear about the crayon on the wall, the lipstick my daughter ate, the money I needed, and that was followed by the bad news about the broken car door. I became a reporter! I forgot that intimacy begins with a warm welcome home and a few minutes for reentry. I became a machine in my home. So organized and performance oriented, that I lost sight of the "let's do nothing" times that build relationships.

A Time for Everything

There is an appointed time for everything. And there is a time for every event under heaven —

A time to give birth and a time to die; A time to plant and a time to uproot what is planted.

A time to kill and a time to heal; A time to tear down and a time to build up.

A time to weep and a time to laugh; A time to mourn and a time to dance.

A time to throw stones and a time to gather stones. A time to embrace and a time to shun embracing.

A time search and a time to give up as lost; A time to keep and a time to throw away.

A time to tear apart and a time to sew together; A time to be silent and a time to speak.

A time to love and a time to hate; A time for war and a time for peace.

(Eccles.3:1-8, NAS)

The world has an expression that "timing is everything." Well, God's Word said it first! In building intimate relationships timing can be everything. However, that requires flexibility. One prerequisite relationship building demands is time. We have all heard that it is the quality of time that is more important than the quantity of time. It is a combination of quality and quantity. Do I give our relationship the time and attention I give other people and other things? I DO NOT have to maintain a schedule that turns my home into a war zone or a pressure cooker. My friend, Ruth, once told a group of young mothers who were overwhelmed at the amount of work they had, to "Just look at one piece of the room at a time and then move right. Soon you will have a made a circle. THEN look at the room!" As wives and mothers we can be overwhelmed when we look for the whole picture to be complete, before we begin to put it together piece by piece.

Schedules are for YOU to control, not TO CONTROL YOU. A favorite sign of mine is one that reads, "Blessed are the flexible for they shall not be broken." Stress and anxiety are caused by unbreakable, overly rigid scheduling. If dinner is late, CREATE diversions. Have a happy hour with your husband and kids, while dinner is being prepared. There's a time to be focused on dinner and there's a time to relax and enjoy your honey coming home. There's a time to play, everyday! There's a time to work and a time to play! If scheduling is robbing you of peace and harmony, what is being won? If your husband gets tied up on the train or caught in cross town traffic, put the pot on low and wait it out. Make his homecoming an event in your day, not an interruption. And if you work and are arriving home late, have a contingency plan. Do the crock pot thing and pre-make dinner. Have a picnic, with some deli sandwiches on a blanket on the den floor. Picnics were fun before you were married, why not now? Be wild and creative. It does wonders for intimacy. There is a time to cry and a time to laugh – what are you doing to create more laughter than crying?

WHEN TWO MULTIPLY

Husbands should be number one on the attention list. It's easy for new parents to allow that little baby to become head of the house. Keep your priorities in God's order. My relationship is with the Lord, then my husband and then the children. Emergencies will always come up – but when I have my priorities set they cannot be shaken, and the emergencies will be taken care of in time.

I heard a young mother tell of how she and her husband had tucked the kids in for the night and were in the middle of making love A little knock came on the bedroom door and a small voice said, "I'm sick, Mommy." The wife was ready to run to the door, when her "about-to-be-deprived" husband barked, "let the little kid barf his brains out!" Emergencies happen! This was an understandable interruption. However, if we allow our children to be the "heads of the house," we are creating a dysfunctional family. There is an order that God has created.

A banner on many marriage weekends says, "The best thing you can do for your children is love their mother!" Children feel secure when Mom and Dad are in harmony. Parents are their children's security. Some of my grandchildren have even mentioned how sad it is for their little friends whose parents are divorced and they can only spend time with one of them at a time. A school project asked the class to draw a picture of their family dinner table. Some of the kids had two tables with a mother at one and a dad at the other. Loving your spouse is the ultimate security gift you can give your children. Assure them that you love Jesus and that means you love their Dad. My friend, Noreen, once told me how she had put her husband's fear of divorce to sleep. He had been hearing of a number of working friends whose marriages were ending in a divorce. Noreen loves Jesus with her whole heart, as well as her husband. She simply said, "As long as I love Jesus, I will always love you. I can't do one and not the other."

We are an electronic society. We can get every marriage course, tape or program right in our own home. We can go away on retreats, marriage seminars or marriage encounters. However, we have THE manual for successful marriage right in the Bible. The problem is we don't follow it. It's old fashioned. We've heard that before, seen it before and we even have the T-shirt. Nothing will make our marriage successful if we don't HEED God's Word. "I foretold the former things long ago, my mouth announced them and I made them known; then suddenly I acted, and they came to pass. For I knew how stubborn you were." *(Isaiah 48:3, 4, NIV)*

We know the answers, we spout the answers, we foretell solutions, but we are stubborn and nothing, NOTHING, will happen or change unless we ACT on what we have learned. We all procrastinate at one time or another. We are stiff necked and stubborn in areas of our choosing. Successful people do the difficult things first.

There is only one, totally effective and comprehensive marriage manual, one sure fire road to success: the Bible. The only problem is we do not act on what it tells us. Let's look at some of these passages and see how they apply. When we apply them, His Word promises a successful marriage:

Wives, in the same way be submissive to your husbands so that, if any of them do not believe the word, they may be won over without words by the behavior of their wives, when they see the purity and reverence of your lives. Your beauty should not come from outward adornment, such as braided hair and the wearing of gold jewelry and fine clothes. Instead, it should be that of your inner self, the unfading beauty of a gentle and quiet spirit, which is of great worth in God's sight. For this is the way the holy women of the past who put their hope in God used to make themselves beautiful. They were submissive to their own husbands, like Sarah, who obeyed Abraham and called him her master. You are her daughters if you do what is right and do not give way to fear.

(*1 Peter 3:1-6*, NASU)

1 and 2 : "Wives, in the same way, be submissive to your husbands so that, if any of them do not believe the word, they may be won over without words by the behavior of their wives when they see the purity and reverence of your lives."

These verses addresses being submissive to your own husband. "Submissive wives" has, in worldly circles, become a curse for women. In Godly terms, it is His plan to provide loving protection for us women. In the scripture it's the order of God. God operates in order. Everything needs a head and God has placed the husband as the head of the household, not in a place of domination or unreasonable control.

The verse talks about an unbelieving husband being won over by our purity and reverent behavior. Pure – without guile, manipulation or a controlling spirit. (The Bible refers to manipulation and control as "the spirit of witchcraft)." Am I pure hearted in my walk?

I will give heed to the blameless way. When wilt Thou come to me? I will walk within my house in the integrity of my heart. I will set no worthless thing before my eyes…

(*Psalm 101:2,3,* NKJV)

Does my husband see one kind of a person in church, or around church people, and another at home? Do I have the same integrity in the kitchen as at a bible study? This verse does not say to walk in integrity in church. It is harder to walk and operate with heart integrity 24/7, in my home. Am I sweet and gentle with others and a shrew when my husband comes home late for dinner? Am I more understanding of other people's failures and the way they disappoint me? Would I talk to the lady in the supermarket more courteously than my husband? Do I preach the Bible at him and have no forgiveness, love or understanding toward him? Do I operate in a double standard mode one for home and one for outside the home?

In short, what does my husband experience at my hand? Am I a "beat you over the head with my Bible" wife? Or, do I walk my talk? Do I mouth off to my kids about their dad, or do I show him respect?

17

Ephesians 5:33: "…and the wife must respect her husband." (NAS) Ever wonder why your kids mouth off to their dad? Ever wonder why they don't say hello to Dad when he comes home from work? Ever wonder why they challenge Dad or question his advice? Could it be that they are imitating you? Do I spend time on the phone gossiping in their earshot? In short, am I exhibiting a pure and reverent spirit or am I just "telling" him what the Bible says? I'm mindful of when my children would have a fight with a friend and tell me all the horrible things that friend had done to them, or how their buddy mistreated them. Next day, they'd be best friends again and I had been contaminated by my child. Do not contaminate your children toward your husband.

"Your beauty should not come from outward adornment, such as braided hair and the wearing of gold jewelry and fine clothes. Instead, it should be that of your inner self, the unfading beauty of a gentle and quiet spirit, which is of great worth in God's sight." *(1 Peter 3:3–4, NIV)*

In the New American Standard 1 Peter 3:3–4 reads a little differently: "And let not your adornment be merely external – braiding the hair, and wearing gold jewelry, or putting on dresses; but let it be the hidden person of the heart, with the imperishable quality of a gentle and quiet spirit, which is precious in the sight of God."

Both translations refer to outward adornment or beauty. The NAS says, "let it NOT be merely external". Both refer to the more important virtue to be the "inner" beauty. The NIV proclaims "your inner self to be the unfading beauty" However, while I totally agree with these statements, I also believe with my whole heart that there is something to be said about "keeping the home fires burning!" Too many of us forget that the first thing that got our husband's attention was probably the way WE LOOKED! Too many of us have become lax in our attention to looking pretty, clean and fairly modern. I am a firm proponent of looking trim, (not skinny, but trim). Too many women use pregnancy as an excuse to retain extra pounds. Age has more to do with weight than having babies, so pay attention to neat hairdos, clean nails, and sensible clothing.. Trim may not be in your genes. Neat is something to be achieved. Sensible, attractive outfits are always possible. Be creative. Even be a little daring. One of my friends played a Halloween joke on her husband. She went out the back door of her house and rang the "trick or treat" bell at the front door. When he opened the door, she opened her raincoat and as she stood naked under it, she said "Trick or treat, Honey."

Many of our husbands work outside of the home. Is the last thing we say to him in the morning as he leaves a command, "Take out the trash!" "Bring home some milk!" "Don't be late!" Do we sleep in, or are we too busy getting the kids ready for school, that we don't even offer him coffee or say goodbye? OR, perhaps, I awake and have forgotten to brush my hair quickly, or brush my teeth? Do we then send off into a world of vultures waiting to devour him? Does he get into his office where a clean, well dressed secretary has the time to ask him how his morning is, or if he'd like a doughnut and cup of hot coffee? I always wanted to send my husband off to his work day, built up, encouraged and feeling loved. I refused to have some other woman smile at him or make him feel more important than I do. ANYBODY can be my husband's secretary or co-worker or car pool companion. BUT, ONLY I can minister to him what he really needs. My husband can have all the friends and buddies he wants, but is he happy he has me for a wife? He can only have one of me! Do I lure him in or turn him off?

P.M.S. DOESN'T MEAN "PUNISH MY SPOUSE"

There is a valid mental and physical problem for women called *pre-menstrual stress*, or PMS. Medical solutions have advanced in relieving many of the symptoms. However, we can sometimes use that situation and embellish on the effects to the point where he (spouse) becomes the victim of "PMS abuse." Some of us can become downright irritable, demanding, and even unreasonable. We are suffering and we refuse to do it alone!

The end of verse 4 says, in both the King James and New American Standard, "…let him see the hidden person of the heart with the imperishable quality of a gentle and quiet spirit." – not boisterous and with contentiousness, not even controlling. A clergyman once told me: "If I can get someone to feel guilty, I can get them to do anything I want." Talk about control and manipulation! If my husband doesn't earn enough money, and I portray the deprived, wanting wife, he'll work harder or longer. If I let him know that this marriage isn't what I expected, he'll feel disappointed. In short, I can usually get what I want, when I manipulate him. A gentle and quiet spirit isn't just my mouth. It's being a contentious woman.

Proverbs 21:19: " It is better to live in a desert land than with a contentious and vexing woman." (NAS) Proverbs 21:9: "It is better to live in the corner of a roof, than in a house shared with a contentious woman." (NAS) Contentious means, "debatable, arguable, unruly, litigious and touchy." Do we ever find ourselves operating in these ways? Am I moody and whiney? Is it all about me and not about anyone else? Is it more important to "prove my point" than to seek the unity God has intended? Is second guessing my husband a rule of operation in our home? Sometimes I ask Ted so many questions, or nag him so much, he feels like he's in court on the witness stand or on the old game show "Twenty Questions."

4 • DESPERATE CHURCH WIVES

There is a show on television named "Desperate Housewives." It's about worldly, spoiled, rich, idle, complaining and frustrated women. These women are conniving, competitive, and more concerned about appearances than they are about relationships. However, I conclude that there are many desperate church wives: spoiled, complaining, worldly, idle, frustrated or gossipy women in our very own ranks. We cloak our complaints, frustrations and gossip in these forms: "Can we pray for my husband?" "I just don't know if I can stay in this marriage." "The man says he's saved, but he never reads the Bible." We talk about them and talk and "share and share" about our husbands. In most cases, we are really just spreading gossip. We are affecting others with attitudes about our husbands even before they have met them.

A friend had told me so many times how her husband just didn't understand her new found faith. He couldn't understand why she had to go to church so much she couldn't cook or clean. I thought the guy was an ogre from the number of complaints about him. (Quite frankly, I think the husbands of Christian wives should eat better and, have cleaner homes and a better love life than unbelievers.) Finally, we met our friend's husband, when he came to serve the homeless on Thanksgiving – one of the sweetest servants we'd ever met. He has since accepted the Lord and is a testimony to the faithfulness of God.

We are desperate for God to move on our spouses, NOW. We have a timetable and WAITING ISN'T ON THAT TIMETABLE! We want a husband who is as spiritual as we think we are and we want it on our terms.

There's more than one group of desperate church wives in the Body of Christ. Desperation isn't just for the woman whose husband isn't yet saved - it's for those whose husbands are saved and not doing what WE think he should be doing. I can attest to the latter in very specific instances. Many wives want their husbands to be the priest in their home, but when he finally takes his right place, they want to keep the robe! "Get saved, honey, but don't rain on my parade."

I have friends who prayed and agonized over their husbands' salvation. One of them got the desire of her heart when her honey accepted the Lord and got very involved in the same aspect of ministry she was involved in. Did she ever get mad at God! After all, she was faithful longer and she had served God more years than her newly saved spouse. She didn't remember the parable about the workers in the vineyard. The owner paid the ones who came first and the ones who came last the same!

Other women, who believe they are called to a particular aspect of ministry, along with their husbands, just get tired of "waiting" for him to get in step. He moves too slowly for the wife. What often happens is the wife "moves out" in the things of God and the husband is left by the wayside.

One very desperate group are those women whose spouses are not saved – yet! Sometimes they are the main stumbling block. Let's look at some very specific scriptures and see what direction the Lord Himself gives to us.

"My soul waits in silence for God only; From Him is my salvation. He only is my rock and my salvation." *(Ps.62:1-2, NASV)*

"My soul, wait in silence for God only, For my hope is from Him. He only is my rock and my salvation, My stronghold; I shall not be shaken. On God my salvation and my glory rest; The rock of my strength, my refuge is in God. Trust in Him at all times, O people; Pour out your heart before Him; God is a refuge for us." Selah. *(Ps.62:5-8, NASU)*

These verses are reinforcing the scriptures from 1 Peter 3. One of the key words mentioned is WAIT. WAIT IN SILENCE. For what? For Whom?

For GOD ALONE!! The very same Psalm, verse 11, spells it out better than I can. It reads, "Once God has spoken, twice I have heard this that power belongs to God!" My glory does not rest on my spouse; it rests on God alone. He is my salvation, my rock, strength and refuge. We are called to trust Him at all times. Pour out your heart to Him; not a prayer leader or pastor or sister in the Lord. OR to your children! Pour your heart out to GOD ALONE. God knows your heart and your MOTIVES. God, in His mercy, is always available to listen. God can bless a mess! He'd just rather bless order and obedience. I will never say it's easy to wait, but God is the sustainer.

For women who are married to men in ministry I have this to share. Some of our desperations stem from the man the world sees and the man I live with. Being marries to a man in the foreground is often the loneliest place in the world and only our God knows the anguish and long suffering that goes on in my heart. I am married to a very strong man of God. I do not doubt that he loves the Lord with his whole heart. Sometimes, however, I think he's so heavenly bound, so supernatural, that he makes my life a whirlwind. I have made the comment that, "Jesus is the LAMB of God. I am married to a cowboy of God"! Different modes of operation! Different personalities! It's very difficult to have someone tell you, "God spoke to me and said…" or something of the like and then for me to disagree. How can I disagree with what God said? How can I say "Could we pray about this?" "Can we talk about this?", when what my husband has heard came directly (according to him) to his ears from God's mouth. I have been at the point on many occasions that I have simply said nothing and waited for God Himself to intervene or to work it out. I learned the truth of the scripture in Psalm 62, "My soul waits in silence for God alone…" There have been many times when I have simply said, "Whatever!" We have probably had more disagreements over things God has told us than any other area of our lives. I have been a desperate minister's wife; a desperate church wife. I have truly found the scriptures in Psalm 62 to be accurate and trustworthy. There has been much comment about my lack of assertion, but I always believed I was in the center of God's will in my faithfulness to my husband. The "lay down and be submissive" thing can

22

be overdone and out of balance too. Eph 5:21: "Submit to one another out of reverence for God." (NIV) God is a God of balance. Submission is part of God's order. However, it is to be a place of protection, not a place of slavery.

We are dealing with self-will, and self-wants and with self-satisfaction. I would hope we will never disagree again or have different opinions. That probably will happen throughout our lives. We will go around those mountains again. However, the good side of this is that we do love one another greatly. We do want to serve God together. We have attained a balance and prayerfully we will stay in that balance. By nature a "cowboy" is a pioneer, a forger of new territory, a person with drive, a survivor; willing to do battle with any enemy. My husband is all of these. In contrast I am quite the opposite. I don't like the unknown. I don't like taking chances or forging new territory. I am too yielding in battle, non-confrontative. I can be easily convinced the other person has the better idea. I fold easily. I am afraid of failure so I don't try a lot of new things. If my husband says, "We don't have any dessert in the house," guess where I head and what I buy.

Now let's take these areas and see how together we can blend a lamb, (Joni) and a cowboy, (Ted), and see resulting growth for us both. When we moved from New York to Florida, I cried all the way to Richmond, Virginia. I liked New York. My family and friends were there. My MOM was there! My security was there. I hated Florida with a passion. I was not a beach person, despised sweat and hated large bugs. I was sure my kids would hate it. After six months we returned to Long Island for Christmas. Driving through the wooded areas of New Jersey with all the barren trees and frosty car windows, I asked my kids if they missed the winter. The comment was made by our oldest son, "It's a nice place to visit, but I love Florida." Score one point for the cowboy. In the following years, we did make good friends, we found a wonderful church family who loved the Lord. We established a successful business. Most importantly, over the years, each of our children received the Lord AND four of our children live in Florida now. They met and married wonderful spouses, all of whom had come to Florida from somewhere else. We do not have to face living here with all of our family elsewhere – four of our children's families live right in the state, no snow-bird syndrome. We live here twelve months of the year and so do our children and grandchildren.

Taking risks – I don't, unless I am "driven" – or encouraged, or nagged. A number of years ago, we opened a real estate office. That was fine until the "cowboy" had an idea that it would be a good thing if I had a real estate license. Well that meant going into unfamiliar territory for me: real estate school and a TEST to qualify. He kept telling me I'd do great and go for it! Trust me, I was very content to have my kids smell fresh baked cookies when they got off the school bus. I was happy cleaning my house and being a contented homemaker. But, my cowboy persisted and in order to get him off the lamb's back, I went to school and got my license. One year later, after I managed the office and learned how to advertise properties, my cowboy, thought it might be a good thing to get my Broker's license. Our office was success-ful, was a ground breaker in our local market and had a good reputation. Why make any changes? Because it made good "business" sense to have two family members with a Broker's license to protect our interests. Well, this little lamb, with God's help, got my Broker's license! The day I took the exam, I felt very prompted to recheck a major portion of the test. I found an error that, when corrected, gave me the necessary points to pass. God had been faithful – not just to the "cowboy", but to the "lamb." We filled in each other's blank spots. It has been years since. When we sold our business, Ted decided not to keep his real estate license. I, on the other hand, thought it would take too much work to redo mine, so I kept it active. Over the years, God has blessed me with a good amount of real estate business. My husband is great at financing, and putting a deal together. I am a real people person and love seeing people blessed in their own homes. Together, the "cowboy" and the "lamb" have found more deals, put together more packages than I would have thought possible. One year we found homes for 5 pastors! We have been able to bless our children and we have been responsible for getting several churches into their own buildings and negotiating for the pastors with government and banking authorities. We do what we do well, and the pastor can do what he does best: *pastor*.

My husband is not intimidated by circumstances or people. When we don't know something or someone, he just encourages me to try, and to try, and to try the new thing. One of the reasons I am writing this book is because he has encouraged me over and over again to do so.

TERROR OF THE TONGUE

The Bible talks over and over again about the tongue. The tongue can be soothing and encouraging. It can also be like a knife, be cutting and destructive. Too often, I have used my tongue as a weapon of mass destruction. We women sometimes, out of frustration, use our tongues and our mouths to try to make a point. When I cannot get through to my husband, or feel intimidated by his intelligence or college degree, I run off at the mouth. At my times of greatest frustration and desperation, I resort to using my tongue. Proverbs is full of instruction about the tongue.

"Better a dry morsel and quietness with it, than a house full of feasting with strife with a fatted ox and hatred with it." *(Prov.17:1, NAS)*

Our homes can be a place of refuge and strength. They can also be filled with strife and anger and bitterness. I can remember making some wonderful dinners and having everything in place for a lovely evening. Then Ted would be late for once reason or the other. The train was delayed. There was traffic on the expressway. A client kept him late. I would stay calm at first, then, I'd start to worry if he was safe. When I'd hear the car coming into the garage, I'd forget about my concerns, and I became irate. Whatever the reason, I bombarded him as soon as he came in the door. It made no difference what I had cooked or prepared. It made no difference how nice I looked or how clean the house was. I had caused strife and changed the nice evening into a battlefield. My tongue had become a terror to my household.

"His mouth is full of curses and lies and threats; trouble and evil are under his tongue." *(Ps.10:7, NIV)*

Is your mouth full of blessing, encouragement and goodness? My husband wants to come home FROM threats, lies and trouble, not walk into a worse mess. Am I providing such a hiding place for him?

"Keep your tongue from evil and your lips from speaking lies. 14 Turn from evil and do good; seek peace and pursue it." *(Ps.34:13–15 , NIV)*

"The tongue has the power of life and death, and those who love it will eat its fruit. " *(Prov.18:21, NIV)*

I have always tried to be an encourager and careful of things I speak into others lives. When one of our sons was young, he could break anything. I used to say to him, "Son, I could put you in an empty room and you'd find something to break." Later because I had repeatedly told him he was expected to be clumsy, he broke some toy of his sister's (actually more than once). When I realized I had been speaking a curse into his life, I repented and then spoke only good things to him. This son of ours is, today, a wonderful husband and dad and he always speaks blessings into his children's lives.

"They continually stir up wars. They sharpen their tongues as a serpent; the poison of a viper is under their lips." *(Ps.140:2–3, NAS)*

There are times, when it's just best to keep quiet. A wrong word at the wrong time can begin a small war between us. Once a word is spoken it cannot be retracted or taken back. Most times these words come out before we know it out of anger in an instant and then we are sorry.

My husband and I have been married over forty-five years. He has been my priority on this earth. We do everything together. One of the reasons we have a great marriage is that we never forgot that we were married to each other, not the children, not the world, not even the church. We have weekly dates – even though we are together all the time. Even if it's a ride to the beach to "breathe in" God's glory and peace in nature, we are enjoying it together. One of my greatest compliments from him, is this, "You keep me close to home, baby!"

MIRACLES IN MY MOUTH

The bible has demonstrated in the above "Terror" verses, the destruction that comes from behind my lips. However, God does not leave us with a problem – controlling our mouth – unless He offers us the solution.

"My lips certainly will not speak unjustly, nor will my tongue mutter deceit. 5 "Far be it from me that I should declare you right; Till I die I will not put away my integrity from me." *(Job 27:4-5, NASU)*

Job decided that he would not speak falsely or unjustly. He declared that he would not act without integrity until he died. The way we bless or curse is a decision!

"My words are from the uprightness of my heart, and my lips speak knowledge sincerely." *(Job 33:3 NASU)*

As the heart is so the mouth speaks. If I have only upright thoughts toward my spouse, I will be sincere in my communication with him. The error of the tongue begins in the heart.

Set a guard, O LORD, over my mouth; Keep watch over the door of my lips. *(Ps. 141:3, NASU)* We can beseech the Lord, to make us aware of the power we have in our words and ask Him to put a door on them.

"Listen, for I will speak noble things; And the opening of my lips will reveal right things. "For my mouth will utter truth; And wickedness is an abomination to my lips. "All the utterances of my mouth are in righteousness;" *(Prov.8:6-8, NASU)*

How much happier would our husbands be if we spoke to them of noble things, reveal right things? Convey good blessings on them.

"Do everything without complaining or arguing, so that you may become blameless and pure, children of God." *(Phil. 2:14-15, NIV)* Having an attitude of gratitude will close the door on complaining and fault finding.

"Rejoice always, pray without ceasing. In everything give thanks; for this is the will of God for you in Christ Jesus". *(1 Thess.16:18, NAS)*

My friend, Harriet, in her upcoming testimony tells us, "If you still have your husband with you, give thanks, appreciate him." Have you thanked him for being faithful and caring for you? Earning a living for you? Being your friend and companion? Being the king of your heart and household? Take time and reflect on his importance in your life. If you have forgotten some of these things, do an inventory of your lives together.

"Hear a just cause, O LORD, give heed to my cry; Give ear to my prayer, which is not from deceitful lips. Let my judgment come forth from Your presence;" *(Ps 17:1-2, NASU)* In an earlier section, I quoted Psalm 62 "In silence I waited for God alone." When we are in the right presence of God, we will see our husbands properly. Being in relationship with the Lord will keep me from deceitful lips.

"Keep your tongue from evil and your lips from speaking deceit Depart from evil and do good. Seek peace and pursue it." *(Ps 34:13-14, NASU)*

God gives an instruction. We make the decision. "Let my lips utter praise," *(Ps 119:171, NASU)*

" Finally, brothers, whatever is true, whatever is noble, whatever is right, whatever is pure, whatever is lovely, whatever is admirable-if anything is excellent or praiseworthy-think about such things. 9 Whatever you have learned or received or heard from me, or seen in me-put it into practice. And the God of peace will be with you." *(Phil 4:8-10, NIV)*

HIDING PLACE

Is your home a place of refuge? When he comes home is it his hiding place, a sanctuary from the world?

"You are my hiding place and my shield; I wait for Your word." *(Ps.119:114, NASU)*

"Be a hiding place to them from the destroyer." *(Isaiah 16:4, NASU)*

"You are my hiding place; You preserve me from trouble;" *(Ps. 32:7, NASU)*

Does your husband feel like your home is his place of refuge – or is it just another battlefield to be won? Does he eagerly look forward to coming home to his castle or is he treated like an indentured servant? He comes through the door and you disappear. Done for the day. Do you drop the kids on him, because you put your time in with them for the day? What kind of atmosphere is there to greet him? Are you on the telephone with a friend and just give him a wave? Are you or your children too busy to greet him? Is TV or the computer too important for you to escape from to tell him you're glad he's home? Does he get a better and warmer greeting from the family dog than from his own family?

While in a bible study a few years back, the leader, a young wife and mother, talked about making her husband's coming home at the end of the day an event! She read in the Old Testament how kings were greeted when they returned home victoriously from battle. They were met by their subjects with banners and flags. She and her girls created a banner and as Daddy was coming home they hung it out to welcome their hero from his daily workplace "battlefield." Her simple act created three great results: 1) He felt special; 2) She had been a blessing to him; 3) She was training her daughters how to be wives to their future husbands.

I always wanted to make my husband's homecoming a welcome worth waiting for occasion. I wanted the atmosphere to be peaceful and inviting. Men work in a battleground. If you're a working mom, you may well want to be the one who feels welcomed, but I believe we women set the atmosphere in the home. It's a gift from the Lord. In Genesis, the Bible says, "Your desire shall be for your husband." Do we show them that we still desire to be with them?

Do we have an attitude of "We" instead of "Me?" Marriage is for a team. The word "TEAM" does not have an "I" in it. I was always conscious of being a hiding place for my husband. The world loves to see Christian marriage crumble. When that happens, there is victory in hell! Others look at their own failures and shortcomings. They think, "Look, even Christians don't make it, and they have God on their side. I guess we're not that bad after all." One of the surest ways for two to become one is being the one willing to die unto selfishness and self centeredness.

"Do nothing out of selfish ambition or vain conceit, but in humility consider others better than yourselves. Each of you should look not only to your own interests, but also to the interests of others." *(Phil.2:3-4,* NIV*)*

These two verses spell "TEAM." Do not be selfish or conceited (think you're better than your spouse). Do you look to satisfy your desires first, instead of the interests of your husband and others. TEAM does not have an "I" in it! A friend of mine makes mention of one of his dad's best counsels: "Give 100%, expect to get some contribution from your spouse, but don't depend on it." In other words, have high expectations of your performance and low expectations of someone else's performance. Leave room for disappointment. But never stop being the one willing to give ALL without anticipation of a return on your account.

5 • KEEP THE HOME FIRES BURNING

GIVER OF GRACE

"Therefore, putting away lying, let each one of you speak truth with his neighbor, for we are members of one another. Be angry and do not sin, do not let the sun go down on your wrath, nor give place to the devil. Let him who stole steal no longer, but rather let him labor, working with his hands what is good, that he may have something to give him who has need. Let no corrupt word proceed out of your mouth, but what is good for necessary edification, that it may impart grace to the hearer." (Ephesians 4:25-29, NKJV)

Grace is good! God has supplied us with an infinite amount of grace to give. Grace in action allows us to overlook failures. Grace is God's gift to us to allow us to be lovers as He is. It makes it possible for us to love one another unconditionally. It is the dynamic that makes it possible for us to see the sinner and not the sin. Grace is the ingredient readily available for us to call on when there is an infraction against us. We call it into play when a person is rude in the Post Office, or cuts in front of us in line, or cuts me off in the parking lot. If we would exhibit to our husbands the amount of grace we dispense to others, we would have much happier lives. We make excuses for other people's mistakes and lack of consideration. I convince myself that the snippy or rude waitress may have had an argument with her husband before work, or maybe didn't get a good night's sleep. Do we make allowances for human error on the part of our spouse? I am more often tolerant of the shortcomings of others than I am of Ted's but, for my husband, there often is no leeway or grace. If someone comes into my home with mud on their shoes, I don't want them to feel badly, so I extend grace. I tell them not to worry about it, but I make my husband feel guilty when he does the same thing. When I have friends over for dinner at a certain time, and they call me when they should already be there, I tell them not to worry about it. Ted comes in late and I become the "slave over the stove" and make him pay with my attitude with every bite of dinner he eats. I have accidents in my house because I'm in a rush. I run late for appointments with my husband. I burn a meal or break his favorite coffee cup! How I love grace toward me when I need it. God, grant me to be a grace giver toward my husband. I want our home to be a house of refuge for him and be his hiding place, his refuge and a sanctuary. A song we sing in church has these beautiful words: *"You're always on my mind. You're all I think of all the time. Draw me closer to you."* I sing that to my beloved all the time. I may not say the words, but I walk them out with grace. GRACE! GRACE AND MORE GRACE free and abundantly available just for the taking.

I cherish each day with my husband. We are good together. We work at being together. We have all the parts necessary to make this machine called marriage a joy ride. We hit bumps, but I surely wouldn't want to be anywhere else.

For many, many years the world has taught the Power of Positive Thinking, and

29

Positive Mental Attitude. I submit to you that God had these ideas first in His instruction in Philippians. We will not be depressed, oppressed, complaining or critical unless we focus on the problems, negatives and wrongdoings. Make a mental decision to concentrate on Philippians 4:8. Praise your spouse, see him as a child of God. Be his "hiding place," his encourager, his friend. "And the peace of God will be with you."

PROVERBS 31 WIFE

"An excellent wife, who can find?
For her worth is far above jewels.
The heart of her husband trusts in her,
And he will have no lack of gain.
She does him good and not evil
All the days of her life." (Prov.31:10–12, NASU*)*

I cannot stress to everyone, including myself, the importance of making your home a magnet that draws your husband home, eagerly, at the end of every day. Create an atmosphere that is inviting and enticing for your man. Make him important. Flame the fire of excitement, romance, and consideration. Go out on a date, even if it's a picnic or walk on the beach. Sit in the living room with your honey, and let the kids watch TV or play a game. Have some fun at home with your man. Share the planning of a night out, or a get-a-way motel visit. Don't overwhelm by planning too far ahead. Remember, when all you wanted to do was spend time together. Don't use money, or the lack of it, to keep you from doing things together. If your car broke down, you would find the money to get it fixed so you could run the kids here, there and everywhere. Make a get-away weekend as important as getting the car fixed. Children learn where they live. Teach your children, by your lives, how GOOD a Christ-centered marriage is.

We can learn to speak the truth in love. We can decide to give our spouses favor with us. We are one. We can be angry, or disappointed or let down, but there is away to talk of it. I always say to Ted, "It's not what you say, honey. It's the way you say it."

We have rarely gone to sleep at night angry with each other. When we have gone to bed angry, we always wake up angry and begin the new day angry. A couple in our church recently celebrated their 58th anniversary and they gave a short testimony that day. They said they never went to bed angry. What's the secret to a marriage of 58 years? "There isn't any secret. Nothing in a marriage should be a secret!" When we do let the sun down on anger, we give the devil a foothold for the next day. The devil can only steal from us if we cooperate and help him.

Suppose one of you had a servant plowing or looking after the sheep. Would he say to the servant when he comes in from the field, "Come along now and sit down to eat?" Would he not rather say, "'Prepare my supper, get yourself ready and wait on me while I eat and drink; after that you may eat and drink?" Would he thank the servant because he did what he was told to do? So you also, when you have done everything you were told to do, should say, we're unworthy servants, we have only done that which we ought to have done. (Luke 17:7-10, NIV)

There are many things I do and contribute to our marriage. We each have our area of expertise – I am very bad at doing the checkbook. If I had checks, I'd write them and not look at the balance. For the sake of our relationship, I do not handle the checkbook. On the other hand, Ted, as intelligent as he is, needs to be instructed on starting the microwave. I do not expect to be thanked for doing what I do well. I appreciate every compliment and every display of gratitude, but I do not expect to be thanked on a regular, moment by moment basis. In fact if I have that expectation, I will be disappointed.

It will be good for those servants whose master finds them watching when he comes. I tell you the truth, he will dress himself to serve, will have them recline at the table and will come and wait on them. (Luke 12:37, NIV)

We need to find these attitudes in ourselves. Strive for the heart of a servant. Brother Lawrence, in the book by himself, *Practicing the Presence of God*, gives tremendous insight to being in the presence of God all the time through his servanthood to those in his monastery. He spent time in communion with the Lord in every task he performed. Lawrence was a servant.

The world teaches us to get not give; be waited on, not wait on others. Jesus, Who was the servant of servants, did only what the Father told Him to do. We expect thanks for the things we are called to do. We particularly want to be recognized for what we do. We may not expect it from the world, but we do expect it from those closest to us. He has given us the grace we need to serve with grace! The servant in the scriptures says, "We have only done what was expected of us."

Let us labor with hands and hearts to give our husband what he needs. Let only edifying and encouraging words of grace come forth toward the man God has placed by my side. My pulpit in my marriage is the most important pulpit in the world. It will have effects going on to the generation next and the ones after that. Many people can touch the heart of my husband, but only I can be his wife.

Our journey has been a long and wonderful one. Like most roads there have been hills and valleys. However, it is my prayer that our road goes on for a long time to come. We have just celebrated our 45th wedding anniversary. When our daughter, Stef, called to wish us a happy day, she asked me "Do you still like waking up next to that same man every day?" More than ever is my answer.

WHEN PULPITS CHANGE

Preachers change pulpits. They get new assignments, move to a different venue. They preach in different places. The PULPIT IN MY KITCHEN can change too. My audience can change, my little congregation can change. Children grow up, go away to school, move to different cities, get married and start their own congregations. Then there is death. Death changes a pulpit. Wives and husband who have been together for many years are separated by death. For many of us, life without a spouse is not thinkable. I scarcely remember my life without my husband Ted. I met him when I was 15. I cannot remember much of my life before that! A friend of mine, who lost her spouse after 30-some years of marriage said this, "In the blinking of an eye, I went from a four letter word to a five letter word. Wife to widow!"

Her pulpit changed! I am so thankful to my Lord that I have not yet had to share this experience. I have however solicited some Godly women to share what went on in their lives and hearts when this ultimate of separations happened. These are precious friends, and Godly women and I appreciate them letting us into the most life changing part of their lives.

HARRIET'S STORY—

When I meet my husband-to-be at a basketball game and was invited out by him and another couple, I went. I am sure he and I believed I was a Christian, as I would have assured anyone I was! I mean, after all, I went to church, knew the right words to say, loved apple pie, lived in America, and had a Mother – I must be a Christian! But one night when I was 16 years old Dave took me to a Billy Graham movie in our city auditorium…I WAS THE FIRST ONE TO RESPOND TO THE INVITATION, meeting Jesus personally for the first time in my life! After Dave and I were married, he chose to go to the denomination he had grown up in; but I was involved and wanted to stay active in my own church. But it wasn't long after our first daughter was born that I wanted us to be with Dave in church; HOWEVER, I SAID TO MYSELF, I will sit on the back row and not 'get involved' with what goes on 'down front' (the altar). But how strange – an evangelist came to town who must have known my life story (the same as any unsaved sinner's story) and I found myself at that altar of grace and mercy. My life changed forever.

I truly enjoyed my husband, my home and my kitchen. Our four children were born over ten years for us to love and care for. And our meals were *always* eaten together at our table. There wasn't even a TV to watch while we ate! My husband entered and graduated from OSU earning a five-year degree during that time, and meal preparation and caring for my family was the biggest part of my life for our family of six, and it was a joy, not a dread, I was a stay-at-home mom who loved every minute of it.

When we were called on by our minister to take in two neighbor girls, it was Dave who finally said, "I guess we can put in bunk beds. We can make room for them in our not so big house. Can you even imagine the joys of always having several girls and boys around my kitchen as I prepared meals for everyone? Was it a joy or a task? You bet it was a task, but the rewards have been joy unspeakable. Sunday nights after church, we would all come to the kitchen starving and what would we have: *Coco Wheats!* Our love for one another was so real because the Lord was so real in all our lives.

Through the years, wonderful grandchildren have been born and grown up and now there is a new little great grandchild. But what wonderful memories I have of those times together at those special meals when everyone was there that I wouldn't trade for anything…and nearly always there was chicken and noodles – homemade noodles made by husband whose presence was always so welcome in my kitchen. But there came a time two years ago when he left me suddenly to be with Jesus, and the kitchen is more lonely now… even all the children and grandchildren could never take his place… but anyone who will, may come to eat with me – there is always room in my kitchen and even with my broken heart which God is healing, my joy in the Lord has never leaked out.

Dave died in his living room, peacefully and quickly. I was in the den on the computer and found him. There are no words to adequately thank everyone for their prayers, hugs and encouragements. If you ever wondered if anyone notices a card or e-mail or words of encouragement, the answer is "Yes, I do." Even this morning, I received an e-mail telling me they are still praying for me as I am here adjusting to what seems to me to be a big empty house. There is no way you can imagine how God can sustain a person moment by moment as He is… and it is just prayer and trusting and believing Who He is. He will return and take us with Him, or we will have an individual departure such as David's – sudden and without warning – even when it is the furthest thing from our minds. I miss Dave so much. You ladies, who have your husbands, treasure them. Thinking of downsizing 49 years of house and home without Dave is pretty overwhelming, but a realization too that the most important part of life has nothing to do with our possessions. I love and praise God, without Him I could do nothing.

Harriet Sanford

March, 2006

RUTH REMEMBERS—

Terry was not only my sweet husband, he was my very best friend, and was for 6 years prior to marriage. I loved being around him, never dreaming some day I would be his wife. I had no clue that I even loved him, which was great!! Love gets you into trouble. When your heart gets involved, it's all over!! After 31 and ½ years of marriage, Terry was tired of fighting for air, and he prayed, "Lord heal me so I can minister for you or take me home". We waited until the last moments of his life for God to perform a miracle and He chose not to, so he waved goodbye to me and said he would see me soon. I was completely lost without my partner, spirit, soul and body. Death is so final that our minds can't comprehend it. It takes the grace of God and time to heal you completely, spirit, soul and body. It took 2½ years of walking in a daze, before I could get a grip on life and any kind of direction for my life. I didn't know who I was outside of being Mrs. Bennett, as I had dated Terry for 6 years before marriage, so was only 12 when he became a part of my life. After going to a crossroads in Hawaii, my heart was healed and the soul ties of my husband were broken off of me and I began a new life in Jesus. I never stopped reading the Word of God, praying and having my devotions, but when your heart is numb, it's hard to hear or respond. The Lord was so patient with me, so loving and kind, and so were people around me. One of Terry's best friends got me a job right after Terry passed away, and it was caring for a 90 year old lady. I poured all my love into that woman and she ate it up. I needed to be needed, and she loved it. My family and Terry's family both have been great. My father took the care of me on his shoulders, as my covering. I could hear it in things he would say and do. My pastor up North who led us to the Lord cared for me as well. I can honestly say I never felt unloved or left out of anything. We were so busy in ministry that we didn't do a lot of couple things so that was not a big issue with me. It was a lot of one on one and then we had each other. I am still waiting for that other to come into my life to share the rest of my life with. I have my 3 children and their sweethearts and 5 grandchildren to love on and be loved by. That is so precious, but it doesn't take the place of a God given partner to have and to hold. The Lord knows what I need, not necessarily what I think I want. He knows what tomorrow holds and he knows my heart, so I will continue to trust Him with my whole heart. He is still the most precious thing in my life.

Ruth Bennett

2006

MARY NELSON – MEMORIES —

In the amount of time it took to say six words, I went from a four letter word to a five letter word. The six words were "There was nothing we could do"; the four letter word "wife" and the five letter word "widow".

My husband, Bob, went to work at 3:00 p.m. At 5:30 p.m. I received a phone call from his supervisor asking if there was someone that could take me to the hospital. My husband had a heart attack and was being taken by ambulance to emergency. My second son, Charlie, and I hopped into the car, leaving Charlie's fiancée and my oldest son, Bran Dee, home cooking dinner. At 6:00 p.m., we were told that there was nothing they could have done. Bob had died.

When death comes so quickly, there's no preparation. Or so you think. You have lost control. You can't blame anyone, no doctor, yourself, circumstances, or God. It's too sudden. I had just turned 57. My youngest son, Billy, still in high school, was preparing for his prom and graduation. Bran Dee was supposed to leave in two days to go back home to Australia. My sons immediately took over the practical aspects, through their grief. My pastor, the elders of my church and their families saw me through the spiritual. We all made it through.

Three weeks after Bob went to be with the Lord, I lost my job. Now I had no income at all and lots of debt and one son under the age of 18. The love of the Body of Christ provided the support that I needed, both spiritually and practically.

Looking back I have been able to see God's hand preparing me for what was to come. A few months earlier, the Holy Spirit had impressed me to memorize the 91st Psalm. I have prayed it every day since. It continually strengthens me. God returned

Charlie from Australia in July the year before, and Bran Dee arrived in October of the same year. We didn't understand what God was doing until it was all over. He kept us in a bubble of Grace. Did I grieve? Yes. Do I miss the intimacy? Yes. I don't belong with singles, and I don't belong with couples.

It is now ten years since Bob went to be with the Lord and he's still a part of my life. When you have children, you always have reminders. And when we are together and reminisce God brings to our memories the good times, and we can laugh about the hard times. Life continues and God is always there. His promise is that He is the father to the fatherless and the husband to the widow. I hold onto that promise. I remind Him of that promise.

Mary Nelson, 2006
Bride of Christ

IT'S NOT SO IMPORTANT ANYMORE

These are some things widowed friends no longer consider to be the major "issues":

" I used to get really mad when he'd leave his empty coffee cup on the table. Now, there's only one coffee cup."

"When I couldn't sleep at night, I'd wake him up to tell him he was snoring. Now, I'd rather listen to the snores and be grateful".

"My favorite words were always, 'Can I get you'; or 'Do you want'; I'd often cop an attitude of 'Why can't you get up and get it?' Now I would gladly act like his puppy do and go fetch anything."

"Football games turned my living room into a stadium on Sundays. Now I would serve hot dogs just to keep him company."

"When he'd make toast, the crumbs would always be left on the counter. Oh, for some crumbs."

"Whenever I took the car, it seemed like the gas gauge was always on 'empty.' I would always moan about being THE ONE to have to fill it up. I'll stand at the gas pump everyday, without complaint, if only my companion was using the car with me."

"Cheering at my grandkids games isn't as much fun as it used to be".

"Eating alone makes me not want to eat."

"I still want to open the door and see him standing there – rather expecting him to be there."

"I never liked how loud he was. Now I wish I had recorded it."

"I was married to Larry for 58 years and it's awful not to have him to talk to."

Just some food for thought: Are the things we complain about or make a big deal of, really worth the effort or energy? We can make so much more of our lives together, if we focus on the treasure we have in our husbands. When I get up every morning, the first words I hear are, "Hi, beauty", or, "Good morning precious love." My husband greets me daily with the same words I can hear God saying to me, His child.

6 • MY LEGACY

*You are our letter, written in our hearts, known and read by all men; being manifested
that you are a letter of Christ, cared for by us, written not with ink but with the Spirit
of the living God, not on tablets of stone but on tablets of human hearts.*

(2 Cor. 3: 2,3 NASU*)*

My legacy is not things; not investments, stocks, jewels or even real estate. My
legacy is people – children now grown into adulthood.

I delight in this scripture because it tells me that my children are my legacy. They
are the gifts God has blessed me with and, they will be my offerings to the world.
Their children and their children form a line that is connected for generations to
come. They will affect the world and impact human beings for ages ahead. There
really is no better treasure to leave my future world. In my opening comments, I
shared how Franklin Roosevelt said that "…mothers are the great national treasure,
doing her part to rear and train the men and women of the next generation."

When we were having our children, I was most fortunate to be a stay at home
mother. I loved it. It wasn't until our youngest son was three that I went to work in
our family company. Times have changed and many young women work outside
the home at jobs their college educations had prepared them for. I found myself saying at times, when people would ask me what I did, "I'm just a stay at home mom."
Almost excusing my inability to "work" I have never really believed that. The world
was in the throes of the Women's Rights movement and it often belittled the stay
at home woman. In truth I believed, and still do, that the stay home mom has the
most important, life changing career in the world. I was (and am) a MOM. Quite
truly there is more work, more labor, more stress and even long suffering, in being
a mom than any position in the world. While careers in the world can be exciting
and rewarding, I believe that most women who have children would prefer to be
stay home moms! When I had my first son placed in my arms, motherhood didn't
seem to present the warm fuzzy feelings I had anticipated at that moment. In fact,
initially, our son was an interruption to my life. However, a mother's love grows to
such an extent that she can hardly "feel" anything separate from her child. I fell so
in love with my babies that I was consumed with oneness with each of them. Every
month I would say, "I love you more this month than last month"– and I meant it!
My children became as much a part of me as my heart, or my arm or my brain. We
were like Siamese twins joined in the spirit.

There is more joy, more happiness and more fulfillment in being a mother than
anything I have experienced in my life. One time, when delivering a Mother's Day
message I wondered what an ad for a Mother in the "Help Wanted" section of the
paper would read: "Wanted full time caretaker, cook, cleaner, laundress, nurse, moti-
vational speaker, driver, class volunteer, babysitter, counselor, preacher, director of

activities. Guaranteed lifetime position, no sick days, some vacation, no holidays off. Very little financial compensation, but eternal rewards and joy unspeakable. The most meaningful position in the world. "

I recently read an article in the paper in a "Dear Abby" column. A grandmother was complaining that her grandson thought all his mother did was "stay home". The column quoted the Census Bureaus figures for 2004 stating that the compensation analysts estimated that stay-at-home moms work an average of 91.6 hours a week and that would amount to a value of $134,121 annually.

In a recent editorial, Kathryn Jean Lopez, Newspaper Enterprise Association, states some of the following: "Some mothers LIKE to care for their children." In her book, *The Price of Motherhood, Why The Most Important Job in the World Is Still the Least Valued*, (Henry Holt & Company, Inc), N.Y. Times reporter Ann Crittenden writes about her own experience, "I imagined the domestic drudgery was going to be swept into the dustbin of history as men and women linked arms and marched off to run the world in a new egalitarian alliance. It never occurred to me that women might be at home because there were children there."

Lopez continues in her press article, "I find it helps to keep in mind a remark Sen. Christopher Dodd,(D-Conn.) let slip back in Nov. 1998 when I (Lopez) want to understand the Sophisticated Mind's view of motherhood. On the Senate floor, he said that women stay at home because they want to play golf, or go to the club and play cards. How about it takes a family to raise a child and they'd like to be there to do that work? That's what most moms who are there are doing at home: Being Moms.

"Americans don't all live on Wisteria Lane (Desperate Housewives). The left (wingers) needs a reality check – to get out and meet some non-desperate housewives. The country is full of them. As a stay at home mom I wasn't desperate, I WAS HAPPY AND VERY CONTENT!"

In an interview a number of years ago, the tennis great, Chris Evert, was comparing winning Wimbledon to being a mother. She commented that winning great tennis matches and worldwide championships was a high that lasted until you had to get ready for the next tournament. She said motherhood was a joy for her all the time.

A 2002 Olympic gold toboggan winner, Vonella Flowers, gave birth to twins after her victory. An article in a national magazine with her testimony, quoted her as saying that "motherhood had increased my faith even more." My faith has never decreased and is still ever increasing as a mother and grandmother. Even with increasing faith and trust in my Lord, I need more. I never run out of a need for more grace either.

My husband and I recently attended a luncheon honoring some of the wonderful, philanthropic members of our community. These 350 people give to the community in the form of libraries, hospitals, volunteering in Big Brother, Big Sister, Pregnancy Crisis centers. They live lives that "Change the World with a Giving Heart."

The Master of Ceremonies was a young husband, father of five and a successful businessman. He opened the meeting saluting the attendees and then proceeded to honor his own mother. "When was the first time you experienced a giving heart? Think of a time when someone's giving literally changed your world." He went on to describe his own birth in a time of national tragedy, mourning and fear for the future. "What kind of a giving heart motivates a woman to endure this pain (childbirth) and uncertainty for a person they have not yet met? To me, motherhood is the ultimate form of charity and giving. Mothers stare a troubled world in the face and then make a sacrifice…for the next generations. As a recipient of that love, I want to say to my mom, thanks Mom for your gift of life. Let us give thanks to all the mothers here for their gifts to the future." There were many moist eyes in the room that afternoon– especially moms!

The role of motherhood is one that is a lifelong role. It begins as we talk to our babies before they are physically here. It continues through the "terrific twos", the rich adolescent years. Motherhood gets tried and tested in the frenzy and furnace of teenage years. Mothers get to sweat out high school, personality changes, and conflicts. They earn more college degrees on their knees than any university can offer. When a son or daughter has a broken heart and lives through broken promises of a friend, mothers carry the pain and suffering twice as much as their child. When the "right person" comes along and a mother can place her child in the loving arms of a spouse, she rejoices and utters many moments of praise and thanksgiving to God. BUT her role is now of continued prayer and ever lasting support. Her crown is not only recognized in heaven, but acknowledged when her children rise up and call her blessed. Recognize, today, dear sister, that God has called us to the highest of callings, co-creator and preserver of life with him

There was a woman we went to church with some years ago. She was a single mother – not by choice – of twelve children. She had a passion for life, God, and her family. A man wrote a letter to our local newspaper and complained about the drain on society that was put on it by "irresponsible people" who kept on having children. He wrote about the burdens large families placed on other members of society. My friend, wrote the nicest, but most profound letter in response to him. Basically, she related how her family had never made a drain on society in any way. In fact, she went on report how in her own family of twelve children many were in involved in community service , the military, education, and so on. None had been arrested and all were contributing to the tax base and the betterment of society. I'm sure this was one of the very mothers that Franklin Roosevelt referred to as a "great asset to her community."

WHEN ROLES CHANGE

The very moment your child is born and placed in your arms, it is the beginning of preparation for that son/daughter to walk off to school, move out for college, transfer across the country or get married. It's a cycle of life. We have often heard someone say that the child is on loan from the Lord, and we need to have the goal in mind of letting go, cutting the strings and releasing the child to the destiny God has already planned for him/her.

We began talking about strong husband/wife ties, which should always be in place, so that letting your child go would not leave you as a couple without a good relationship.

Parents need to be depended on and children need to be prepared to be independent. We never let go of them spiritually and emotionally. We still pray daily and more so for our children and grandchildren. We are part of their lives, want to be, and can never have enough time with them. However, when we give them the proper roots, we can be assured they will have strength in their wings to find the right direction.

Years ago we started to pray for the spouses our children would eventually marry. A friend once told me, "Don't just pray for a Christian spouse for your kids. Pray for God's highest and best, the perfect partner for each of them." That was a good piece of advice. There are many "perfect" looking people out there. There are nice, good looking, young single people with great family ties and maybe even rich young people in our church surroundings. However, if you have a strong willed daughter who is dating a "whimpy" young man, you could be witnessing a disaster in the making. Our children need to be encouraged to "wait on God" for that right partner. This is the time to pray, not express your doubt or disapproval.

Once the partner has been "discovered", we as parents need to change our position for the attentions of our son/daughter. When their children come along, that position changes again. Being a grandparent puts us in a third row seat. Life does become a fulfillment of the song *Cats and the Cradle* – it seems as if kids always want more time from mom and dad, while mom and dad have jobs and responsibilities that can limit "kid" time. Then it changes and the parents, now older, have the money and the time, but their sons/daughters are burdened with the demands that keep them busy and preoccupied. Now the younger parents are trying to make ends meet, juggle chores, go to ball games and ballet practice, and the cycle repeats itself and begins all over again.

When children begin to marry, Mom, your tent enlarges. You no longer have two children, you have four adult children. When you are blessed with five children, as we are, your tent now contains ten! Consequently, we're challenged with different personalities, needs and gifts. Time to change again. Life is full of changes.

In the section on husbands, I alluded to the leaving and cleaving that must take place for the "two to become one". It is vitally important for parents to ALLOW their child to leave the home, and encourage them to become one with their new spouse. Children (adult) need to be given the freedom to establish the new home and family on a solid foundation, without the interference of "Mom and Dad". Unsolicited advice can be toxic.

Do not compare your new son/daughter to yourself. Do not point out how "we did it this way." Do not put guilt trips on them when they meet the needs of their spouse before you. Do not "insist" they have dinner with you every Sunday. Do not put them in a position of choosing you over husband or wife – you will lose and that you should. Spouse comes first. Do not become a "smother" mother. Perhaps the greatest adjustment I have ever had to make is letting go. You will never stop being concerned for your "child" or "grandchild." You may even be told not to worry – but we do. Motherhood does not stop when your "child" is married. Emotions cannot be turned off like faucets. There are times when I feel like my husband and I have just each other. Children grow up into adults, married adults, adults with children. My input has changed and it is a constant reevaluating process.

Our family always had big get-togethers on holidays – especially Christmas and Thanksgiving. Even after there were new husbands and wives, we had those holidays together. Then one of our married daughters and her family started to go "camping" on Thanksgiving, so that old gang of ours seemed to be put on the back burner. When I spoke to her, this is what she said, "Mom, you always taught me that what Daddy wanted was your first priority. Well, now my husband and the boys want to go camping, and you taught me well. I need to please MY family first." She was absolutely right, and I am to this day very proud of the wonderful wife and mother she has become. As a side benefit, just the other night her husband, a most wonderful son, said, "Mom, thanks for your daughter," the sweetest words a mother can hear. So, while I had to let go, I have gained so much more back. I have to say I love that young man more today than I did 20 years ago! If you choose to hold on too tightly, to your married children, especially by employing guilt trips, I can guarantee you will alienate them. I have done that and it is very painful. I also have learned that what I consider attention or helping can be viewed as interference or smothering. Seek The Lord!

Never encourage your adult child to gossip about his or her spouse. Never conspire with your child to "…keep this between you and me, and don't tell your husband or wife." I learned that I don't want to hear anything, IF I'm told not to tell my husband. It's divisive and attacks unity in your household.

Instead, always find the good. Lift your adult children up to their kids, especially when the grandchild is complaining about Mom or Dad. Show great caring and respect for the spouses of your offspring. Just like you need to be a different mother to each of your birth children, you need to be able to become a different mother for and to their spouses. Know your limits and boundaries. Know which home you can "just drop in on" and which you need to call first. Allow them to set their rules of operation and blend into those situations. Know when to become involved and wait for the invitation.

A friend of mine asked me how I could let go and I told her that I never really let go, I just let them be about what God has for them to do. Actually, the more we let them direct and set their own guidelines, the more our families want to be around us. Wait for that phone call that says "We need a little help or counsel here." Respect their homes. You do not have the right or freedom to just come over whenever it suits you.

You do not have the right to have a key to their house. All things must be mutually agreed upon and respect is a two way street. If you want to be treated as King and Queen by your family, try treating each of them as princes and princesses.

INTERFERE OR INTERCEDE (as a Mother)

We need to be very protective of the relationships of our sons/daughters and their spouses. Many mothers, in particular, take on a hurt attitude when their children marry. They make demands on the newlyweds' time, phone calls and visits. Sometimes even what I have done out of my personality can be seen as interfering. I like to do spontaneous things – a surprise party, making a meal for my busy daughters, or just dropping in unannounced. Each married couple in our family is different and I am not always mindful of the needs of each. Today, so many young marrieds work and they do not need an overbearing, complaining mother-in-law to interfere with their new marriage. The Bible talks in the Old Testament about a newly married man in "When a man has taken a new wife, he shall not go out to war or be charged with any business; he shall be free at home one year, and bring happiness to his wife whom he has taken." *(Deut. 24:5–6, NKJV)* Too many mothers and fathers just can't allow the adult child to get firmly planted in their marriage, before they keep the old demands in place or bring on new demands. Things and relationships change.

When we were first married, it was a foregone conclusion that we would have EVERY Sunday dinner at the home of my husband's parents. We worked all week and Saturday became just another work day trying to cook, shop, do laundry and get to know each other. We made a promise in those pressure years not to put our children in this kind of a position later on. On holidays both families "kept score" as to whose turn it was to have us. The constant battle to balance and keep everyone else happy made for pressure-filled celebrations. Parents can be downright unreasonable. We try not to "bother" our married children on weekends, when it is their time to refresh and build a healthy home life. Notice, I said, "try", because we fail at times. What seems to work for us is making ourselves available and open to participate in any activity, they want, but allowing them to initiate the invitation.

We are important in our family's lives. We know that, but we are secure in Him. We chose not to INTERFERE, but rather to INTERCEDE for them. We pray daily for our children and their children. We ask God's guidance and protection as spoken of in Psalm 91. We also ask for a multiplication of His grace and mercy. We pray for wisdom for them, and we pray unity in their homes and hearts. We pray for wisdom for ourselves.

BASKET CASE

One of my favorite accounts in the Bible is in Exodus 2 and 3. One year I was preparing to bring a Mother's Day message and was going to do the "standard" thing – Biblical Mothers. Once I began and came to the Moses account, I saw some very new revelatory things. First I noted how the midwives "greatly feared God" and would not kill the Jewish baby boys as Pharaoh had commanded them. These were relatively unknown names to most Christians, Puah and Shiphrah. They were obedient to God and the Israel grew to be mighty in number and in strength. "So God was good to t he midwives and the people multiplied and became very mighty. And it came to about because the midwives feared God that He established households for them." *(Exodus 1: 20-21, NAS)* These midwives were actually mentors and substitute mothers for the babies of Israel.

One of the babies saved was the son and daughter of the house of Levi:

Now a man from the house of Levi went and married a daughter of Levi. The woman conceived and bore a son; and when she saw that he was beautiful, she hid him for three months. But when she could hide him no longer, she got him a wicker basket and covered it over with tar and pitch. Then she put the child into it and set it among the reeds by the bank of the Nile. His sister stood at a distance to find out what would happen to him. The daughter of Pharaoh came down to bathe at the Nile, with her maidens walking alongside the Nile; and she saw the basket among the reeds and sent her maid, and she brought it to her. When she opened it, she saw the child, and behold, the boy was crying. And she had pity on him and said, "This is one of the Hebrews' children." Then his sister said to Pharaoh's daughter, "Shall I go and call a nurse for you from the Hebrew women that she may nurse the child for you?" Pharaoh's daughter said to her, "Go ahead." So the girl went and called the child's mother. Then Pharaoh's daughter said to her, "Take this child away and nurse him for me and I shall give you your wages." So the woman took the child away and nursed him. (Exodus 2:1-9, NAS)

The mother of Moses hid her child for three months in order to keep him alive. She was a woman from the house of Levi, a believer. She trusted God and when she could no longer hide her son, she prepared to "send him off" to keep him alive. The bible says she got a basket and covered it with tar and pitch. Tar and pitch are dirty and sticky materials. You cannot apply them unless you get your hands dirty. Being a mother means getting your hands dirty; diapers, clothes, sticky problems, mediating disagreements, fighting some relationship battles.

However, the mother of Moses put him in a basket and did not take him out. In fact the person who watched over him was his sister.

Mothers cannot be there 24/7 and the One Who is able to be a watchman is the Holy Spirit. There will be times in the lives of your children that you can only entrust them to God. My daily prayers – even now – are that God give His angels charge over them.

There will also be times when, like Moses' mother, we will want to take them out of that dangerous basket they are in for the moment. Had she taken him out of the perils of the Nile she may very well have interfered with the plan of God for his life. Mother's may think they are rescuing a son or daughter by doing the school projects for them or defending them in situations where the child is wrong. Teachers in schools, coaches on Little League teams, even policemen and authority figures, have seen the wrath of a mother who can never hear or see her child corrected. A friend of mine tells of an incident when her kids were in the car with an adult who deserved, and got, a traffic ticket. Her sons came home and ranted on about the "rotten cop" who gave the driver a ticket. Needless to say they viewed policeman differently and without respect. If you do not teach your children respect for authority, bail them out of every problem and scrape, I believe you are not equipping them for life as a responsible adult in an adult world. So, it may mean they don't pass a class or even have to go to summer school. If they slack off or do not do what they should, there will be consequences. You are abusing your child if you continue to do everything for them. You may also be interfering with the very plan God has for them.

When our 19 year old son was injured in a construction fall and was paralyzed from the waist down, we would have traded places with him to "save" him from this tragedy. WE WOULD HAVE INTERRUPTED GOD'S PLAN FOR HIS LIFE. That accident rescued him from a lifestyle that may have cost him, not only his legs, but maybe his life. God has THE PLAN. Today our son is a pastor in a church of several hundred, has a wonderful wife and three awesome kids. All to the honor and glory of God.

When our youngest son was in elementary school he wanted to ride his bike to school. I knew I would say, "No!" I wanted him to go on the bus to "be safe." I was, at that time, a "smother mother." Only I could protect him. After all he is the baby in the family. I deferred to his Dad to keep me in balance. He rode his bike to school. I prayed. He came home to tell me of an incident on the way home. The kids were riding when a school bus stopped to deposit some kindergartners off at the stop. One little guy dropped his pencil in the stairwell of the bus and reached in to get it. The driver did not see him and he started off with the little one caught in the door. The point is that GOD protects your children on the bus or on the bike. The 5 year old wasn't hurt, but scared.

When our daughter went off to college I thought it was around the world. It wasn't. It was another state. God took care of her. When she took a job that was on the other side of the world (my opinion), I felt more assured she was in God's hands. She met and married a wonderful man there and they have just added to our still growing family.

When one of our kids just couldn't get past World History in college, we said forget it and go on. This one is now a successful business person.

If you make excuses for you truant child, addicted child, traffic violator child or rebellious child you may be setting them up for a life of torture, a time behind bars or even a life on welfare. Irresponsible children and unaccountable children tend to be the same when they reach adulthood.

There is an expression, "You have to pay the piper." WE cannot skate through life on the coattails of another. One of the saddest things we can experience is to see a forty or sixty year old man or woman what are still being treated like mommie's little girl or little boy. What happens to that unequipped "adult" when the parent dies? It is not the order of God for grown adults to be treated and acting like "children." There is a season for all things in God. There is a time to hold on and a time to let go.

Marriage is a time to let go. When our oldest daughter got married, we had a wonderful wedding. Our new son's family lives in the same town, so our family had truly been extended. (It's great to have all the grandparents at a little league ball game!) Anyway, the celebration with both families was great. After the newlyweds headed off for the honeymoon, we went back to our family home with the rest of our adult children. When the evening was over and the final goodbyes were said, my husband and I waved them off and stood in our living room. We had always left our front light on until the kids came in from a date or night out. This night, my husband shut off the light and I heard a sniffle in the living room. When I asked him what was wrong, he said, "No more lights for Stephanie." An era had ended and a new era had begun. She had left our home, but not the team and never our hearts. In fact, she has added to our already large family a glorious array of new faces, and personalities in her husband and two fine sons.

Welcome your new sons and daughters into your "family". Embrace them and you will never, ever, lose a son or daughter to marriage. You will instead, increase the size of your tent and the size of your heart. Your pulpit may have been relocated, but you'll never forget your first place of ministry. Instead of your pulpit in your kitchen, you now have a traveling ministry, the homes of your adult children, and a portable pulpit that can come with you.. You have instead become a "church planter", by sending out a new "preacher" to a different location, to reach the world with the gospel of Jesus Christ. Our married children have a direct influence on the friends and families of their children. Some of our families NEVER have just their family in the house. They always have an extra kid or kids over. When they do the visitor comes to church with them if it's Sunday. Sometimes the kids go home and bring their own moms and dads to church. It's "family evangelism."

GRAND TO BE A GRANDMA

There's a bumper sticker that says, "If I knew how great it was to have grandchildren, I would have had them first." I do not feel that way. I love being a mother. I was the mom who got upset when the summer was over and the kids went back to school. I liked when we had snowstorms that meant we were housebound with hot chocolate and no phones. It meant the world kept away! However, when we got the phone call that our first grandchild, Hannah, was on the way I was ready! Then, some months later came another call. Our precious Theo was born. Since then some more weddings, and some more phone calls, for a total now of 11 with #12 on the way. One year there were three new grandbabies, each one more exciting than the last. More joy was spread throughout the family. If I have one complaint about being a grandmother, it's that I never have enough time with them, but I never will. We do have an abundance of time, but grandmas get selfish! It's just the way life goes on.

I am not through becoming a grandmother and I have learned a great deal, but

I surely do not know it all. I have learned to pray for them, enlarging my spiritual tent. I have tried to learn not to smother them and to let mom and dad be mom and dad. I am not the mother, I am the grandmother. I told one of my grandsons one day that I loved him and he answered back, "love you too, Grandma." I said why do you love me and his answer was a sweet, "Cause you're my grandma, and you are always kind and nice to me." That's all I need. I love their giggles and smiles and see their wounds from time to time. I see them growing faster and faster and I always want to keep up with them. One of my grandsons makes me feel like Wolfgang Puck. He says. "Grandma, you make the best meatballs in the world." So the next thing I do is make Drew more meatballs.

As senior parents, we have learned to respect the ruling authority in the homes of our sons and daughter. I do not think that we are interfering grandparents. Of course, I have gone beyond boundaries. I repent and go on to my next error in judgment. We strongly abide by the rules of their home.

We strongly avoid the statement, "When you were little, we did it this way!" No two homes have the same schedule, but each one works and works well. We have been truly blessed with great mothers and fathers for our grandchildren. We want always to support their rules and regulations. One sure way to avoid conflicts is a boundary list. Knowing what is acceptable or not is half the battle. If they can't have soda or ice cream or must do certain chores, we respect that. Should we have the occasion to have them overnight or go on a field trip with them, then, we become a temporary authority. We believe strongly in having a very major role in our grandchildren's lives, but we are not the parental authority.

INTERFERE OR INTERCEDE (as a Grandmother)

One of the greatest opportunities to bless your grandchildren comes through prayer. We pray for our grandkids, for their schooling, learning, relationship with God, their jobs, their sports. We try to be vigilant, keep our eyes and ears open. We ask the Lord to show us what may be disturbing and help us, with wisdom to direct our footsteps. Today, especially with blended families, children grafted in may have heartbreak we do not know of. If we develop a personal relationship with each child, become a student of them, we will see things that the Lord wants out in the open. Children may be afraid to bring some things to a parent's attention, but a grandma who has a warm heart and opened arms may be the place where that child will come for comfort and direction.

As Grandparents we try to go as many games and concerts and Grandparents' Days as we can. We always want to be there for our grandkids and we love every minute of it. We want to see them graduate, to drive their first car, get their first license, or go to their first prom. When they first begin sports, we go, are just entertained and laugh and laugh.

We also recognize that having them overnight or over for supper isn't always a gift in the lives of their mom and dad because of schedules. So, we who have time on our hands sit in the stands and cheer them on and get to visit mom and dad at the same time. In short we try to lighten the load, not add to it. As a result, we don't stay home and watch TV as much, but do get out and drive to games more often. We see the friends of our grandkids growing up right before us. We see the newest generation becoming the next generation and we find a way to cherish each minute.

We have set in our hearts to be friends, encouragers and supporters of our grandchildren. "If you're not part of the solution, you may well be part of the problem." Be sensitive. My husband and I are blessed to our socks when we witness what good parents we have in our family. We salute them as fine men and women of God who are contributing to the Church and their community and raising a high standard of excellence. Is there a greater Legacy? We think not.

MIRACLES IN YOUR MOUTH

One of the greatest gifts we, as mothers and grandmothers can offer is the gift of blessing with our mouths. Parents necessarily need to be in the role of authority and discipline. Mistakes kids make, poor grades, bad decisions are not the end of the world, although they sometimes feel like it. Parents have several areas in the lives of their children where they must continually uplift or edify a child. Grandmas have the opportunity to turn bad into good, hopelessness into hope, mistakes into opportunities to try again. Whenever one of my children or grandchildren has a need in their lives, that child becomes my favorite for the duration of the problem. It's especially important to tell them that although they may have failed, they aren't a failure; they may have made mistakes, but THEY are not a mistake.

It is especially necessary to be longsuffering in these situations, not interfering, but praying, and being available to talk or touch. A child who has difficulty in school can labor over homework, projects, tests, etc. Recently I was reading a book which addressed the child who struggled day after day in school. That child is not a weak child. The book mentioned how much courage it takes for a kid to go into that classroom day after day, remembering the failure of the day before, and the days ahead. BUT, the courage comes in going back day after day! I cried and cried. One of our grandchildren was having great difficulty. We realized her battle was not just the books. It was a battle of will and of sticking to it, and she had withstood that! I've never been prouder of her! She's like the kid who keeps coming back on the basketball court after losing a bunch of games. Lesson learned here, "I am not a quitter and I will be a success." Become a student of your grandchildren as well. Some of them like to have a special secret friend to open up to. Wouldn't it be grand to be that person?

The scriptures talk about the importance of "input" in our lives. "I have been reminded of your sincere faith, which first lived in your grandmother Lois and in your mother Eunice and, I am persuaded, now lives in you." (2 Tim. 1:5, NIV)

Timothy's father was not a believer, but the sincere faith of his mother and GRANDMOTHER transferred to Timothy, not just faith, but sincere faith.

Can we leave a better legacy to our grandchildren than to impart to them the faith we have in God and His perpetual love and concern for them? Mother, father, grandmother can only be part of their lives for so long. God is their eternal partner, protector and guide. In Psalm 91 we read:

He will call upon Me, and I will answer him; I will be with him in trouble; I will rescue him and honor him. With a long life I will satisfy him and let him see My salvation. (Ps. 91:15-16, NASU)

I believe the Word of God with my whole heart. Let me end this chapter, saying that the promises of God in Psalm 91 assure me that God will answer the child and grandchild that call upon Him. He will give angels charge over them, when we cannot be physically with them. He will be with them in all trial and tribulation and time of danger. Whether things look bright or dim on the path or the way they seem to go, it is only temporary. The Bible says to teach them the way they should go and they will return to it. My Lord promises to rescue them and even honor them AND grant them His salvation. We can stand on the total truth of God's Word. We serve a very faithful God. We operate in the power of The Holy Spirit.

We can begin knowing our child as soon as our baby is conceived. We can talk to, sing to, pat and rub that child before we ever see it. Positive talking, terms of endearment are heard from the womb. Today, with so many knowing the sex of the child before birth, we can talk to the baby by name. Instilling images of goodness into a baby, images of their value to you as a mother and their value as a child of God will affect that child after it is born. Likewise, negative comments can give a child lifelong struggles of non acceptance. If a child feels rejected by a parent it is often a basis for thinking no one else sees your worth. We need to be pupils of our children, and in order to do that we must know our child. We can teach our child many things, but we first must know them.

My friend, Phyllis, taught me this lesson many years ago and I have passed it on innumerable times. She was a pastor's wife and a teacher in their church school. She had six children of her own, but no experience as a teacher. I asked her how she was doing it. Her answer was : "For the first two or three weeks of school I don't try to teach them anything. I fall in love with them, and they fall in love with me. Then I can teach them anything." Powerful advice. Become a student of who your child is! Then you can teach them anything.

One of the most valuable nuggets of information I ever got on being the best mother and teacher of my children I could ever be was from another mother of five. I had two small sons at the time and was overwhelmed at her ease with her brood. I asked her how she did it and she said that it wasn't the physical work of cooking, cleaning, driving and nursing that was the work. The real work was being a different mother for each child. Kids aren't cloned! If you have two kids, you need to know them individually and specifically. If you have five children, you need to be five different moms! No two children are completely alike. They have different moods, temperaments, different likes and learning abilities. Don't major on the minor with kids. Major on the major. One time I found a plaque that I bought as a reminder of what the important things in my dealing with my children are. It read, "Clean your room. Cut the lawn. Do your homework. Please get a haircut. P.S. I love you." All of these things are valuable. However, the "P.S. I love you." should come first.

Treat you family like a team — not a gathering of individuals who want their own way. Let me elaborate. I never made different meals based on likes or dislikes. I didn't cater to whims or spoiling them. I did, however, recognize that some of them were morning people, or night people. Some of them needed no help with homework. Some did. I had self starters and those who needed to have their batteries jump started. One son heard instructions once and proceeded. The other did the job, but I had to be right next to him. One of my kids would take clean laundry and put it away and another would put the folded wash right back in the laundry hamper. I never needed to ask who did certain things, because I already knew. The being a different mother for each child is part of knowing their emotional, physical and spiritual make ups. All of your children may be a lot alike, but be wise to the fact that they are also all very different. We begin to "know" our children as we walk and talk and eat and sleep with them. Knowing my child begins before they are even born. I can begin bonding with my child when he/she is still in the womb.

I was a very young bride and an even younger first time mother. All I ever wanted to do was be a wife and mother. It was my Cinderella fantasy – "to live happily ever after." I've had a few abrupt awakenings over the years. I anticipated being June Cleaver with Ward by my side. I would always happy, always perfectly neat and prim. Linen napkins every meal. Dirty dishes that did themselves. I never imagined not having glasses or silverware that didn't match. Never conceived the idea of being late for appointments, getting up in the middle of the night, or getting a phone call from the school nurse in the middle of a lunch with a friend. I never anticipated not being able to finish a meal without sharing it or giving up a dessert when some little folk wanted a second helping. My "lived happily ever after" came in the midst of these interruptions to life!

I come from a family where you NEVER, EVER discussed pregnancy. I had many questions and was afraid to ask. Therefore, each day taught me something. I learned as we went along. I was a young mom and I used to comment to people, "I grew up with my kids." One of my biggest wake-up calls came while being wheeled down the hallway to the delivery room. I can remember as clear as today, saying to myself, "I don't want to do this!"

My next "hello there" episode came when I realized my 6'3" husband thought of my son as a competitor. All the time I had for him was now to be shared. First time mothers, like myself, jump at every sound the baby makes. I thought my baby would vanish, if I didn't stand over him and watch him every second. It's good to learn early on that WE can NEVER be there all the time. Only the Lord can watch over my children all the time, all the time. If he fussed when I put him in his crib, I'd be fast to rock him. Guess what! He liked being rocked and so he got used to it, something like an addiction to a sleeping pill! So, dinners would be late, or laundry not folded, and my neat and orderly world became a thing of the past. At least temporarily. My honey was used to laundry ironed and folded, and dinner cooked on time. He liked sleeping late on Saturday mornings. We liked going out without remembering we needed a babysitter. Things had changed. After so many years of being somewhere and having a phone ring, and expecting the babysitter, I still hesitate at a friend's house when I hear the jingle of the phone. I forget, I don't have babies or babysitters any more!

Things in life just would get settled and here comes another change. When our second son came along 18 months later, I had already set the routine up and now had to learn to adjust. I had learned that the baby can wait a bit, or cry a bit. Babies do not like being out of control. Babies may be tiny and fragile, but they don't melt away if their diaper isn't changed immediately and they don't stop talking to me if I don't run at the first sound of a cry.

You can be a good mommy with God at your side. Ask Him. He'll show you how!

Before I formed you in the womb I knew you, before you were born I set you apart.

(Jer. 1:5, NIV)

For You formed my inward parts; You wove me in my mother's womb. I will give thanks to You, for I am fearfully and wonderfully made; Wonderful are Your works, And my soul knows it very well. My frame was not hidden from You, when I was made in secret,

And skillfully wrought in the depths of the earth; Your eyes have seen my unformed substance; And in Your book were all written The days that were ordained for me, When as yet there was not one of them. *(Psalm 139:13–16, NASU)*

God, the Creator, has woven us perfectly, formed all the inward and outward parts. Science today has come far in understanding the human body, but the Creator is the Lord. He formed us perfectly, whole and well working. He has placed in each of us His Image and Likeness as well as many gifts and talents. He Himself is the architect of all humanity.

Being made in the Image of God, we possess many God-like traits. I will only identify all the good traits in my son or daughter when I truly know them. Since God is our heavenly Father, we inherit from Him every good gift and character.

"Then God said, 'Let Us make man in Our image, according to Our likeness; and let them…'" *(Gen 1:26,NASU)* Once the decision was made , God created Adam: "Then the LORD God formed man of dust from the ground, and breathed into his nostrils the breath of life; and man became a living being" *(Gen 2:7, NASU)*

When God created Adam, He created the perfectly sinless man, because God Himself was without any sin or blemish. We have all inherited traits, talents, personality, and temperament from our earthly parents. More importantly, we have the character of God, our heavenly Father.

However, when Adam and Eve, our first earthly parents brought sin into the Garden of Eden, they altered our inheritance to now include a sin nature.

"Behold, I was brought forth in iniquity, And in sin my mother conceived me." *(Ps 51:5 5, NASU)*. The iniquities of Adam and Eve have been passed through the generations.

"You have not heard, you have not known. Even from long ago your ear has not been open, Because I knew that you would deal very treacherously; And you have been called a rebel from birth."*(Isaiah 48:8-9, NASU)*

In the Word of God the scripture tells us we were brought forth in iniquity and sin – left over from Adam and Eve. God Himself says in Isaiah that we have been called "rebel" from birth. We have two natures – God and Evil.

"The rod and reproof give wisdom, but a child who gets his own way brings shame to his mother. When the wicked increase, transgression increases; But the righteous will see their fall Correct your son, and he will give you comfort." *(Prov. 29:15-17, NASU)*

The Word tells us that we are rebels from birth. Eve became the first rebel when she disobeyed God and ate of the forbidden tree. Adam was a rebel when he relinquished his authority, knowing God said NOT to eat of that tree and he turned a blind eye when his wife went against God's command. In Isaiah the scripture clearly says that, "…you have not heard, you have not known. Even from long ago your ear was closed."

"Now the serpent was more crafty than any beast of the field which the LORD God had made. And he said to the woman, 'Indeed, has God said, "You shall not eat from any tree of the garden?"' The woman said to the serpent, 'From the fruit of the trees of the garden we may eat; but from the fruit of the tree which is in the middle of the garden, God has said, "You shall not eat from it or touch it, or you will die."' The serpent said to the woman, "You surely will not die! For God knows that in the day you eat from it your eyes will be opened, and you will be like God, knowing good and evil." When the woman saw that the tree was good for food, and that it was a delight to the eyes, and that the tree was desirable to make one wise, she took from its fruit and ate; and she gave also to her husband with her, and he ate." *(Gen 3:1-7, NASU)*

Look, for a minute, at what transpired here. The crafty serpent approached the woman. Her first mistake was to even consider LISTENING to him. She "entertained" him! Sometimes we women are easily misled. We know the Word of God and we sometimes doubt Him. Eve began to doubt as soon as the tempter began to tempt! She followed the leading of her senses, "The tree looked good to eat and looked pleasant." She didn't even think, or stop to pray. She made an emotional decision. She ate! Then she drew her naïve husband down with her. Thus sin entered the world, and we were forever subjected to the Adamic nature in Man.

Adam and Eve chose NOT to listen to God and instead followed the voice of the serpent. It was the first time in the history of mankind that man chose NOT to trust God, but to trust more in what he wanted instead. The first man and woman opted to challenge God and they did. The first sin was disobedience and it was motivated by selfishness. The root of all sin is selfishness.

When we brought our first son home from the hospital, I was quite happy. However, immediate waves of bonding and overwhelming love eluded me. I was anticipating this wild and passionate devotion to my baby. My life seemed to have gone from easy going, easy does it to "is this what it's all about?" My uninterrupted sleep was gone. Eating a meal from start to finish became a luxury. Going to the bathroom or taking a shower was no longer a privacy moment. Our beautiful nursery was now looked on as a place where someone came to visit and stayed for over 20 years. As I surveyed the diapers, and extra laundry pail and sat in the dark with a crying baby at 2 AM, I wondered if our home had not turned into a war zone. Him against us – and he was winning.

I would have totally rejected the idea that this beautiful bundle of peacefulness had a sin nature! However, he wanted to eat when he wanted to eat, cry when he wanted attention. When his diaper was dirty, he let me know NOW! His little world was himself! He had every adult in his life as a captive audience. Babies are born with a survival instinct, and that's good. But they also control much of their environment. We need to recognize the "natural" tendencies of children in order to train them in the way they should go. We also need to search for our child's gifts and talents in order to "Train up a child in the way he should go, even when he is old he will not depart from it." *(Proverbs 22:6, NASU)* Always keep in mind that each child is an individual in all areas of their life and training.

Many of our traits are inherited from generations before us. While many of our strengths are inherited from descendant family members, so too are our iniquities. Ambition, drive, intelligence, and attitudes are all inherited. Temper, anger, rage, addictions, flaws in our character are also often passed down.

In the Bible we see examples of falsehood being manifested in Abraham in Genesis 12, when he lied to Pharaoh out of fear. He told the ruler his wife was his sister because he was afraid he'd be killed. Then Pharaoh could take her for himself. In later stories in the Bible we see how his son, Isaac deceived Abimelech *(Genesis 26:7)* and had a proclivity toward lying, inherited from his father, Abraham.

Eve was a strong willed and controlling woman. She wanted to be like God! She took Adam down with her. Sarai couldn't believe God for His promise of a child and she spoke to Abram and said, "Please go in to my maid; perhaps I will obtain children through her." *(Genesis 16:2, NASU)* Rebekah convinced her favorite son, Jacob, to deceive his father and steal his brother's birthright. *(Genesis 27)*

Sin, iniquities are passed down through the generations.

"You shall not worship them or serve them; for I, the LORD your God, am a jealous God, visiting the iniquity of the fathers on the children, and on the third and the fourth generations of those who hate Me, but showing loving-kindness to thousands, to those who love Me and keep My commandments." *(Deut 5:9-10, NASU)*

When we accept Jesus Christ as our Lord and Savior, we shed the nature of Adam and take on the nature of Christ. This is the same for our children. In the meantime, we must apply Biblical standards in rearing and raising them. The bible talks in "Train up a child in the way he should go, even when he is old he will not depart from it." *(Proverbs 22:6, NASU)* We are told specifically that we are to "train up" our children. To "train" means to teach, coach, educate, instruct, guide, tutor and school our children in many ways. The most important training we can offer is to train our children up in the ways of the Lord. In order for us to successfully do this we must 1) know Him personally and intimately ourselves, as Lord and Savior, and 2) know our child personally and intimately. I can only share my personal relationship with God and His Word if I have first hand knowledge of Him and His Word. says it much better than I can, "The things you have learned and received and heard and seen in me, practice these things, and the God of peace will be with you." *(Philippians 4; 9,*NASU*)* I can share what I have learned and received.

We must instill in our children a love for the Lord and for His principles and instruction. We must encourage them to have, and develop, a personal walk with Jesus Christ, for He will guide them into all truth. There are very valuable lessons that we can teach our children, but we must also walk our talk.

When our youngest son was young, we used to read books together and then discuss them for his book reports. He is my Huckleberry Finn child! Living in Florida he loved to fish and play and play and fish. We would read the scriptures and pray at night. Our favorite scripture is "Whoever speaks, is to do so as one who is speaking the utterances of God; whoever serves is to do so as one who is serving by the strength which God supplies; so that in all things God may be glorified through Jesus Christ, to whom belongs the glory and dominion forever and ever. *(1 Peter 4:11,* NASU*)* I used to tell him that no matter what he did with his life, his whole life, even if he was a waiter, to excel and do it with all his might to bring honor and glory to God. Well, he became one of the best waiters around and learned how to be a servant. He's no longer a waiter, but he is still a servant and he indeed brings honor to his God. Something as simple as reinforcing God's Word on a regular basis has formed this young man into a fine human being.

People sometimes get caught up in the "empty nest" fear syndrome. I had on my refrigerator for many years, a magnet from a dear friend, Roberta. It said simply, "Two things we give our children. One is roots and the other is wings." Mom, let me say this to you, train your child in the way he should go and in his older years he will not depart from the ways of the Lord. He may stray a bit, but be assured he will return to the ways of his God. Any child who has good roots will be able to fly and prosper in all things.

Perhaps, the most difficult part of parenting God's way is to be consistent in the rules, persistent in the ways of God and steadfast at all costs. Prayer is essential and will undoubtedly last a lifetime. I am continually seeking God's face for direction as a mother. The bible gives direction on one of the ways to train a child in "He who withholds his rod hates his son, But he who loves him disciplines him diligently." *(Proverbs 13:24,* NASU*)* The world today is running scared of disciplining a child physically, but the Bible tells us that withholding the rod of discipline translates to hating our child. Children will learn to respect authority and follow rules, or they will suffer the consequences. We either learn to discipline ourselves or we are inviting the discipline of another person or agency. I can choose to obey the speed limit, discipline myself, or be corrected by a person in uniform riding in a car with a blinking blue light on top.

As a necessity for the right performance we need rules and regulations in our homes, clearly defined rules and boundaries. We must be very precise in our guidelines. " Simply let your 'Yes' be 'Yes,' and your 'No,' 'No'; anything beyond this comes from the evil one." *(Matt 5:37* NIV*)* I have found when I am not clear and direct, yes or no, I leave the door open for interpretation. "Maybe" can cause tremendous misunderstanding. Example: If my daughter wants to sleep over a friend's house and I say "I'll think about it," and I don't say yes or no, I've said "maybe". What she heard was what she wanted to hear which is "Yes." We cannot take a "MAYBE" approach. Each person in that situation has heard what he/she wanted to hear. Rules and boundaries are for a reason. Learning to live by the authority set over you as a child will train you for living in the real world.

There is a way to use the rod of correction correctly. Select a "rod" – we had a ping pong paddle. Some people use a wooden spoon. The most important thing is that the rod not be a hand – your hand. The rod is not you! Not a part of you. Always remember wisdom is key. Never administer the rod of discipline in the midst of anger, or when you are too emotionally distressed. Oftentimes that's when excess prevails unnecessarily Always explain to your child why they are being disciplined. Children often say, "You're punishing me." No, son or daughter, when you know the rules of behavior and YOU decide to break those rules, you are asking me to discipline you. Responsibility for a child's actions or inactions should be placed firmly on the child.

The most important part of disciplining with the rod is, when it's all over, hold your child and reinforce your love for your child. Just like God, our Heavenly Father, we can object to the sin, but cradle the sinner in arms of love and acceptance.

Children like to be "waited on." One of the most valuable areas of schooling we can give to our children is teaching them to be responsible. Answering to authority is a priority area. Being part of a family "team" is paramount in teaching children to pitch in and work for the common good. Mostly in families we should learn there isn't any such thing as a "free ride". Our daughter had some chores that needed to be done around the house and yard. She gave out the assignments to her two sons. One of them, on hearing his lawn task asked his mom, "What do I get for doing it?" Her answer was, "How about supper?" Respect for other members of the family and respect for the "common living areas" shared by the rest of the clan are all part of the training that becomes a lifetime lesson. Sharing and caring for others is a very valuable lesson in life that begins in the home. Spoiled, demanding, bratty little kids grow up to be spoiled, demanding and bratty adults. The world exists today with an "all about me" attitude. That is the opposite of the message of Jesus Christ, Who said, "I have come that they may have life, and have it to the full." *(John 10:10, NIV.)* The New American Standard: "I came that they may have life, and have it abundantly." *(John 10;10, NASU)*

One of the greatest teachings to family members, especially children, is to remind them of what Jesus came for. It's not all about them. It's about reminding them of how pleasing it is to the Father when we bless one another. A family is a team and "TEAM" is not spelled with an "I" in it.

Children who learn responsibility at home will be more responsible outside the home. Cleaning, tidying, helping with chores, putting clothes away, putting toys away are all tasks children can and should participate in. I have never been in favor of Moms picking up and putting toys away when kids are done with them. If they mess up, they pick up.

The Bible says "For even when we were with you, we used to give you this order, if anyone will not work, neither let him eat. For we hear that some among you are leading an undisciplined life, doing no work at all, but act like busybodies. Now such persons we command and exhort in the Lord Jesus Christ to work in a quiet fashion and eat their own bread." *(2 Thessalonians 3:10-12, NASU)* Can an instruction be any more clear than this?

On a Christian Broadcast Network show, I once saw a show on work ethic among young people. They were conducting interviews near the beach in Ft. Lauderdale, Florida. Many of the young people interviewed didn't even know what a work ethic was. It was explained as a standard you set in your workplace. Some of the kids said they didn't work because, "they expected me to work on weekends!" Others said they had worked, but it was summer and they needed a day or time off. These young people had obviously not been "trained to toil." Some of them didn't realize that to buy food to eat you must have money earned by toiling. "Cursed is the ground because of you; in toil you will eat of it all the days of your life." *(Gen. 3:17, NASU)*. Right in the beginning, as soon as man fell, God foretold the history of man, telling him that he would eat of the ground, if he toiled. The Bible tells us to toil and to work.

Children who are in school must understand the concept that at this time in his/her life studies are to be toiled, worked at. Lessons need to be prepared in advance. Moms, you do your child no favors when you do the work for them. You do them no favor when you do their science project. You do not help them when you go running off to WalMart for construction paper or special folder for that book report at the last minute. You should not "bail" your child out for his/her lack of attention to assignments. You can get him/her an assignment book, review the assignments with them and help them plan. BUT, DO NOT cripple your child or smother your child by doing his/her work. Where will you be when Johnny or Suzie has to take a test in school, or give a report in the boardroom? Train your child to think and reason on his/her own. I know of cases where mothers actually buy a duplicate set of teacher's manuals, so son or daughter will have a "jump" on the school year, because the child wouldn't self-start. The son /daughter knew Mom would bail them out and the Mom made all the sacrifices to drum the lessons into the kid's head. Mom was finished with school. Mom had a good job! I call these mothers, "smother mothers." No favor is done for child or parent. The child grows up to be a quitter, because he/she had never been encouraged and disciplined to "toil."

Our son had a basketball coach in high school. I learned one of my most valuable life lessons from him. He was a new coach at a high school that had enjoyed a winning basketball dynasty forever and ever. That winning coach retired and this new fellow came on board. He began his first year without many of the starters from the past victorious year. He had a big order to follow and the team just did not win any games. The coach and the team became unpopular with the fans. Soon some of the team members began to fall by the wayside and quit. The coach called a meeting of the surviving team members and their parents. He went on to encourage us all and said this, "I am so proud of these young men. They come back week after week, do their best and still don't win. To come back when you're getting booed and then to come back again shows me the character of these guys. I want you to know, it's not about a basketball game. It's about life. Do you hang in there when the going gets tough? Do you keep coming back to work when your job and boss aren't what you had been promised? Do you just hang it up, quit, and move on to try something else? Basketball games aren't won or lost in the last minutes or seconds of the game. Like life the way you play the game from the beginning is what will determine if you are a winner or a loser." We've lost track of Coach Trainor, but we haven't lost sight of his powerful message to parent and child. Winners are those who toil, those who give up are often not willing to toil.

Spiritually, we need to encourage our children to seek a personal relationship with the Lord. "Toil" after His Word. Study to show yourself approved. Educate them on seeking the Lord through prayer, the Word. Develop good attendance at church and youth activities. Encourage them in their choice of right and wrong, good and evil.

I have said this before and will probably say it again and again because I so strongly believe it: "Two things we give our children, one is roots and the other is wings." If the foundation is good, the structure will likely stand

"Unless the LORD builds the house, they labor in vain who build it." *(Psalm 127:1 NASU)* The Lord must be our firm foundation. We must exhibit our faith and beliefs to our children in word and in deed.

A number of years ago, I was diagnosed with breast cancer. The most difficult thing for me was to see the concern in my children, along with their fears. Then I told my associate pastor, at the time, that I was really sad that my kids had to go through the trial and be worried about me. His response to me was, "Well, Joni, it's a way of building faith in them. You can't build their faith. They have to walk it themselves. Just remember, without a test, there isn't a testimony." I rejected this thought as being a cruel way for God to do it. No mother wants to see her child suffer or worry. But it was the truth. God was faithful and I have been healed. My children saw the faithfulness of God firsthand. They have had to trust God in many instances: finances, a spouse, sick kids, a job that is lost, a house destroyed by a hurricane. They have seen better jobs come after a lost one, healthy children. They have wonderful spouses, and even have children provided by God through adoption from around the world to fill their homes when it didn't seem like it would happen. Faith is built and developed in the toil of our lives.

When we are confident that we have taught all we can teach and laid the groundwork AND trusted our children to the Lord, we can be assured that they will fly with the eagles. They will find their way. My favorite Psalm is 91. It has been my daily prayer for my husband, children and grandchildren for many years. I refer to it as the "Parent Prayer."

He who dwells in the shelter of the Most High will abide in the shadow of the Almighty. I will say to the LORD, "My refuge and my fortress, My God, in whom I trust!" For it is He who delivers you from the snare of the trapper and from the deadly pestilence. He will cover you with His pinions, and under His wings you may seek refuge; His faithfulness is a shield and bulwark. You will not be afraid of the terror by night, Or of the arrow that flies by day; or the pestilence that stalks in darkness, or of the destruction that lays waste at noon. A thousand may fall at your side and ten thousand at your right hand, but it shall not approach you. You will only look on with your eyes and see the recompense of the wicked. For you have made the LORD, my refuge, Even the Most High, your dwelling place. No evil will befall you, nor will any plague come near your tent. For He will give His angels charge concerning you, to guard you in all your ways. They will bear you up in their hands, that you do not strike your foot against a stone. You will tread upon the lion and cobra, the young lion and the serpent you will trample down. "Because he has loved Me therefore I will deliver him; I will set him securely on high, because he has known My name. He will call upon Me, and I will answer him; I will be with him in trouble; I will rescue him and honor him. With a long life I will satisfy him and let him see My salvation."

(Psalm 91, NASU)

I have prayed this prayer daily for many years. I have prayed it with confidence since I believe my children dwell in the shelter of the Most High God, since they have become born again. He is their refuge and fortress and they can trust in Him above all else. Read this psalm carefully. It says all any mother wishes for her family. He is their protector, ALL THE TIME. It is not possible for me to be with them 24/7, but my Lord is. Calamity and dangers may be all around, but the psalmist says, "it will not come near their tent." No evil, or plague. He will send a host of angels to be "concerned about all your ways." Our children will be exposed to some "lions and cobras, (not good things) and some "snakes" Perhaps not literally, but in other forms. However, God says, "Because he (I say "they") have loved Me, and called upon my name, I will answer him; I will be with him in time of trouble; I will rescue him and honor him. With long life I will satisfy him (them) and let them see My salvation." Everything, we as mothers could want for our children is in the promises of God. His Word has given us the words for a complete prayer request.

There were times when my children would have a bad day, or a friend or teacher hurt them. Times when they'd fall and get hurt or cut. Times when they were sick or greatly disappointed. There were challenges at every turn, high school and college papers due, tuition needed, difficult decisions to be made, choosing a life partner, staying up with their sick kids or just watching them play sports or drive the car for the first time. Lions and cobras and snakes come in all forms. I could never imagine them all. Therefore, I put my trust in God and asked Him to keep them in the shadow of His wings.

The book of Proverbs chapter 18, verse one in the New American Standard reads, "He who separates himself seeks his own desire. He quarrels against all sound wisdom". In the *Amplified Bible* it reads a little differently: "The person who lives alone is self indulgent showing contempt for those who have sound judgment." The difference between a single person and a family is that the person alone needs only to be concerned about himself/herself or maybe a cat or dog. Basically they set their schedules. If they want to eat at 6 o'clock, that's great or eat at 4, that'll work too. If they awake at 7 AM in the morning, that'll fit into their schedule. If they sleep in until 9 or 10, it doesn't interfere with anyone else. All a single person has to do is consult with himself or herself. In a couple, or even more so in a family, there are other people to consider, other schedules to consider, the needs of other people to be concerned about. That's why a family must be a TEAM. The main consideration is not "I", but "we." Sharing is the only way your team can be coordinated and work like a well oiled machine. Sharing must be learned because we are all selfish in our own way. Even an infant wants what he/she wants when it's wanted. Sharing is a biblical principle and it is basic to the giving messages in the Bible: reaping and sowing, reaping and sowing. Learning to share opens the door to giving. Both must be taught and learned.

"Instruct them to do good, to be rich in good works, to be generous and ready to share." *(1 Tim. 6:13, NAS)* "And do not neglect doing good and sharing: for with such sacrifices God is pleased." *(Heb. 13:16, NAS)* "Be devoted to one another in brotherly love; give preference to one another in honor, not lagging behind in diligence, fervent in spirit, serving the Lord." *(Rom. 12:10, NAS)* We serve the Lord by serving others.

From early childhood we begin to teach our children basic manners and respect. There is an acceptable mode of behavior that is no longer emphasized in the home first. "Do nothing from selfishness or empty conceit, but with humility of mind let each of you regard one another as more important than himself; do not merely look out for your own personal interests, but also for the interests of others." *(Philippians 2:3-4, NAS)* Learning to be respectful of others must start in the home. Brothers and sisters learn to share and to give right at the dinner table or in front of the television. Common areas of the house – kitchen, TV room, bathrooms, play areas are common areas and we should teach our children to be neat and orderly in favor of family members. Saying please and thank you, excuse me or I'm sorry should be common expressions in our vocabulary. Basic and simple rules of kind behavior start at home and then spill over and become a standard for the way we act outside. These few things are the beginning of learning how to be a giver, which is a Godly principle. Jesus died to Himself and is our teacher on how to do it. He is the ultimate Giver; He gave up His seat in heaven to come to earth, as a man. He gave up the riches of heaven to live on this earth. "For you know the grace of our Lord Jesus Christ, that though He was rich, yet for your sake He became poor, that you, through His poverty might become rich." *(2 Cor. 8; 9,* NAS*)* He gave up heaven for earth so we could inherit the Kingdom of God. We argue about what television show to watch, or who plays with the toy first! We must learn the basics of giving "things" before we will ever learn to give our time, our services, our help or our money. God is a God of sowing and reaping, "Remember this: Whoever sows sparingly will also reap sparingly." *(2 Cor. 9; 6,* NIV*)* Sharing with others begins at home where even the most basic sharing is tested. Often times we are more giving to those outside of our homes.

As a small child, our oldest daughter Stephanie was the ultimate sharer. She never had a problem giving her toys to brothers or sister. Often the toy would not come back in the same condition it was offered. She used to be "trapped" into telling her two older brothers bedtime stories about Jack and the Beanstalk. In Stef's version, Jack didn't go to "the market". Her Jack went to the deli! Her brothers would fall asleep and she would, dutifully, still be telling her tale to herself. To this day she is the most generous and giving person. She's always there to take someone's kid overnight or make a meal or spread the need for prayer. She is a tremendous testimony, as is her family, of the generosity of God here on this earth. She believes in the principles of sowing and reaping. When someone is sick, she sends a dinner – a full course dinner not just a fast food one. She includes treats and dessert. Their family home is a playground for her children's friends. She and her husband are always having kids over and over and over. "Enlarge the place of your tent; Stretch out the curtains of your dwellings, spare not; strengthen your cords And strengthen your pegs. For you will spread abroad to the right and to the left." *(Isaiah 54: 2 and 3a,* NAS*)* There's always room for one more at their table. There's always a place where an air mattress can be put down for friends to sleep over. The Bible tells us to enlarge our tents and spare not. Share! There will always be enough food and space. Our son and his family have "movie night" and a bunch of kids gather at the Campo house for a night of fun and games. The Bible speaks of sowing and reaping. We never knew exactly how many people would be at our dinner table, but God always performed another "loaves and fishes" thing and we always had leftovers. When we give out generously, we will always have more than enough. God truly loves a cheerful giver. "Heal the sick, raise the dead, cleanse the lepers, cast out demons; freely you have received, freely give." *(Matt. 10:8,* NAS*)* "Now this I say, he who sows sparingly shall also reap sparingly; and he who sows bountifully shall reap bountifully. Let each one do as he has purposed in his heart, not grudgingly; for God loves a cheerful giver." *(2 Cor. 9: 6-7,* NAS*).*

Children learn by what they live with. My niece, Kim, was recently writing a check out for a donation and when her girls asked what she was doing she told them what it was for and they each said, "Can I give you five dollars to send for me?" Children learn from their experiences in life, home, school, church and social surroundings.

My mother always used to tell me that when I was giving something away it should be something in good condition. If it was trash, it should go to the garbage. If you clean out your closets and drawers, make sure the items you're donating are clean and mended or don't give them at all. Give a gift that is a gift, not a throw away.

One time someone made our family a meal at the time of a death in our family. The problem was she wanted us to drive an hour to get it and then come back home another hour. My son said to me, "A favor isn't a favor if it causes too much inconvenience." If I truly want to bless someone, it shouldn't cost them anything. Think your giving through and truly let it be a blessing to another person.

When we start to give of ourselves by sharing and caring, doing nice things for someone, it will be easier to give of our money. God calls us to be cheerful givers. The Kingdom of God must have the gospel spread throughout the world. Airline companies don't give free tickets just because YOU have a message from God. Hotels aren't free. Think of the missionaries who have been serving in the field and away from home. They need prayer support, but they also need monetary support. We cannot be sending and not giving. As a little girl in a religious school we were given "mission boxes" to save up for missionaries. We learned to be givers when we were young and we still give.

We cannot outgive God. "Will a man rob God? Yet you are robbing Me! But you say, 'How have we robbed You? In tithes and offerings. You are cursed with a curse, for you are robbing Me, the whole nation of you! Bring the whole tithe into the storehouse, so that there may be food in My house, and test Me now in this," says the LORD of hosts, "if I will not open for you the windows of heaven and pour out for you a blessing until it overflows. Then I will rebuke the devourer for you, so that it will not destroy the fruits of the ground; nor will your vine in the field cast its grapes," says the LORD of hosts." *(Mal. 3:8-11, NAS)* Not only will our blessings be poured out to overflowing, but God will rebuke the devourer for you. The world has a saying : "The rich get richer and the poor get poorer." God's Word says, "Give and it will be given to you, good measure, pressed down, shaken together, running over, they will poor into your lap. For by your standard of measure it will be given into your lap in return." *(Luke 6:38, NAS)* God will bless us for our generosity to others, whether it would be finances, love offerings, meals, gifts or even time. We don't give to get, but God will honor us. In Matthew 14, there is an account of the disciples coming to Jesus and telling Him to send the people to the villages so they can get something to eat. Jesus says, "They do not need to go away; you give them something to eat". They replied; "We have here only five loaves and two fish." *(Matt. 14:16, 17, NAS & NIV)*

The Lord took the little and multiplied it so that there was more than enough plus leftovers! We all have something to give. Look beyond finances. How about a smile to the checkout lady in the supermarket? How about helping someone whose car is stalled in the parking lot? How about helping an old person load their groceries? How about giving some cookies or flowers to the crossing guard at your kid's school? Go and volunteer at Meals on Wheels and bless a shut-in. We all have SOMETHING to give. One of the greatest blessings you can give to a person in a nursing home is simply your presence. Your visit can light up their day and they become uplifted. It costs nothing, but yields much. Your reward is a heavenly one.

A WORD ABOUT DEBT AND WISDOM

Recently, I was chatting with our granddaughter. We were talking about her oldest cousin taking me for a ride in my car since she now had her license. She wanted to know if Hannah had a car. I said she had a job and was saving up for a car and insurance. She thought for a second and then responded: "Why does she have to save?" In her secure world where all of her needs are met at 8 years old, she has not yet developed the concept that we have to pay for "stuff" with money. Teach your children fiscal responsibility and money principles when they are young. When they are old enough, teach them about money, purchasing, saving and giving. To provide for them is one thing. To "give" them everything will put them into shock when they enter the outside world. Allowances are beneficial. Saving up for something they especially want is also good. Teach them to spend what they have and not get in debt. You are the best example to them in the way you live. Is it within your means or are you always playing catch up? The Bible teaches us about debt. We are told to "owe nothing to anyone except to love one another." *(Rom.13:8, NAS)* "The borrower becomes the lender's slave." *(Proverbs 22:7, NAS)* We must pay back when we lend. The Lord forgives our debts, man doesn't – he expects to be paid back. Macy's, Target, Sears, restaurants, airlines all expect to be paid.

One year my niece got a note home from school regarding her daughter. The teacher said they were withholding her final grades – 2nd grade – until the child had satisfied her cafeteria "debt". When her mom questioned her she told this story. Seems one day Alex ran out of money at lunch and the cafeteria worker told her she could "charge it." It was so simple that when she wanted an extra ice cream or treat after that day she just said. "Charge it"! It was so very easy. Her end of term bill was $10 or more. Her mom asked her why she did it and was reminded, "You charge all the time." Mom told her that when you charge something it just puts the payment off, BUT you must pay. When charge card offers come in the mail, I automatically cut up the card and throw it away. I have had struggles over credit in the past. Saving is one of the disciplines in life. Either we discipline ourselves or the bill collectors will discipline us. Teach your child the difference between "I want" and "I need." I recall a young woman telling me she really needed a particular item. When I asked if she needed it or just wanted it, her reply was, "Let's put it this way, I want it so badly that it has become a need!" I was in a department store with our daughter one day looking at all the new fashions for spring. After a while she said to me. "Mom, let's get out of here I'm beginning to lust after all this stuff." Wisdom in finances and discipline in life are basic Biblical principles.

Over the years I have, as a Licensed Realtor, had young people wanting to buy homes. Somehow they forgot that they owed college loans and simply stopped paying on them. They had graduated and were making money, but didn't see any reason to pay back the government for their education. Wrong! Their credit scores were poor as a result. Debt must be repaid. There is a need to prepare your child for life in the world. Mom and Dad do great disservice to a child when they give them a free ride and fail to teach them responsibility.

As a Christian we must be more responsible in all areas of our lives. At work, do we give our highest and best performances? We should be the best and hardest workers in the office and marketplace. We need to know WHOSE Name we carry. A show I saw on CBN was talking about work ethics. A number of young adults were being interviewed on Ft. Lauderdale Beach in Florida. For the most part they didn't know what the word meant and asked the reporter to explain it Some of the comments were so pathetic, it was sad. A few said the things they wanted most in a job were good pay, good hours and no work on weekends. All of those jobs were taken, so it was off to the beach. As mothers, we need to instill Godly ethics in are children. The best way to accomplish that is by being a good example and a good steward. Hard work yields good benefits. Paul says:

"For even when we were with you, we gave you this rule: "If a man will not work, he shall not eat." We hear that some among you are idle. They are not busy; they are busybodies. Such people we command and urge in the Lord Jesus Christ to settle down and earn the bread they eat. And as for you, brothers, never tire of doing what is right." *(2 Thess. 3:10-13, NIV)*

This message was to the church – believers. We are well instructed here; no work, no food, some are lazy (no work ethic), spoiled (Mom or Dad do it all), and meddlers. "Idle hands are the devil's workshop." Be diligent. Never tire, never give up or in. Instruct your children. There are no free rides in life. If it sounds too good to be true or sounds too easy, it probably isn't good or easy.

One of my favorite stories comes from our daughter. It was summer and her sons had been given a list of daily chores, more than usual. She was telling them to go out and do some yard work and she was getting some resistance. Her oldest son said, "Okay, and what do I get for doing the yard"? Very quickly she answered, "How about dinner?"

Family is sharing and caring and responsibility. It means pitching in and being part of a team. What we learn at home is what we live by. It means giving to one another, supporting one another.

We would always go to all of our youngest son's basketball games. We'd cheer and cheer and they rarely won. In the course of many games we'd encourage him to "take the shot!" He almost always passed it to another player. At the end of the year he got the award for the most assists in the season. He gave it away and he got the award for the most assists, the best giver.

Let me close this section on giving and taking, sowing and reaping, sharing and caring with this:

At the close of our school's basketball season "gifts" were willed to each team member by the cheerleaders.

One son received the gift of "Most Devoted Family" for the noticeable presence and support received from his family throughout the year. Not a lot of victories for the team, but a lot of support for a brother and son. What was being done here was not about winning the title, but about giving and sharing in the good times and in the bad. It's about being a family. Life isn't "all about me." If it is that way, then it's time to revaluate. Giving and sharing begin at home.

Time With You, Is My Way of Life

I have found a way to commune with the Lord everyday
When I do my laundry, I fold and, I pray.
I thank You Lord, we have clothes to wash and fold
I thank You Lord for healthy bodies that I can hug and hold.
I even thank You for all the chores and all the work
I Praise You for all the mess, dust and dirt
I thank You for every tiny pant and shirt or skirt,
I know footprints on the floor mean healthy, running feet.
Without these marks of life, I'd not be complete.
I can even rejoice in the linens and the sheets
So, while I have so very, very much to do,
I can find time to spend with You
So with every sheet I fold
There is a blessing to be told.
In every thing I can have a Love Song
Thank You Lord for having me where I belong!
And when my house is very quiet, clean and neat,
I think of all my years of work and remember them as a treat!

There is so much work involved in caring for a family. I have been blessed with finding ways of doing things that have turned my efforts into prayers and my work into worship. I have had many good models and wise women speak into my life.

One of the most frustrating "jobs" I do is dust. It seems like throwing feathers into the air. When I dust, it flies away and lands right back. One Sunday our pastor was encouraging us to "Rejoice always; pray without ceasing; in everything give thanks; for this is God's will for you in Christ Jesus." *(1 Thess. 5:16-18),* NASU) So I decided to try it for the week – dusting and praising! For that week, and since, whenever I dust, especially pictures of my family, I begin to dust with an attitude of gratitude. I would dust my many pictures and pray for the face in the frame. I became so aware of the gifts of people God had placed in my life that I forgot about the dust that came back down. It was just another opportunity for future "dusting." My attitude had changed when I looked at my work as an opportunity to serve and an opportunity to focus on my blessings. I would think about the person in the frame and I would pray and thank God for that special person in my life. I'd take a minute and think of a fond memory or moment that was special with each face.

Instead of grumbling that I had to clean my bathrooms, I rejoiced that I had bathrooms and indoor plumbing. Instead of moaning that I had six sets of linens to wash, I praised God I had six people to put in those beds at night. When it came to folding laundry, especially those little baby clothes, I would act like Peter in, "God was performing extraordinary miracles by the hands of Paul, so that handkerchiefs or aprons were even carried from his body to the sick, and the diseases left them and the evil spirits went out." *(Acts 19:11-12 NASU)* I would fold my laundry, piece by piece. I literally "Laid hands" on each piece and prayed for the one who would wear it. When I made the beds, I would smooth out the sheets and pray for the little (or big) body that would occupy that territory at night. I actually enjoyed folding and making beds.

Another opportunity that I rejoiced in and gave thanks for was when I was preparing meals. I thought about the many mothers whose children would go to bed hungry that night, who may never have ice cream to offer for dessert. I would then pray for those mothers. I would prepare my meals with thanksgiving and joy. I always looked forward to all the faces around my table, thankful that I was "Not alone, ("It is not good for man to be alone"). I would be happy that I could anticipate happy faces, sharing our family meal around the table at the end of our day. One of our sons would walk home from the school bus with his friend. On one occasion, our son commented that his friend, David, had made the comment, "I can smell your mother's kitchen."

One of our daughters commented to me one day that she had made chicken salad for her husband. She related how it made her remember how I was happy making chicken salad for her dad when she was younger. She said she was happy for the opportunity to be making something nice for her man. I love serving my family. I see it as a reward from the Lord not to be alone.

I rehearsed an attitude of joy and gratitude, and as a result, my life was filled with great love for my family and thanks to God for blessing me so much. My mother used to turn a problem into an opportunity to be thankful. When I would complain about a broken dishwasher or broken car, she'd simply remind me how good God was that I even had those things.

When my children were very young I didn't have a quiet moment, even in the bathroom. My mom would tell me how quiet it was in her house now that we siblings and my dad were all gone. She'd caution me not to say, "I'd give anything for some peace and quiet." "Someday you'll willingly trade your peace and quiet for activity and chaos." She couldn't have been more right.

Now, our home is always neat and clean and tidy. Company can drop in anytime and I'm ready. But how I miss the fingerprints on the bathroom mirror, the big wheel in the driveway and I even miss the permanent magic marker on my table. I sorely miss the noise and the constant ringing of the phone. I miss the squeals of delight and even the occasional shrieks that come with having five kids all over the place. Enjoy all of this, young mothers, time waits for no woman.

One of the most important times in family life is the time when they break bread together. Jesus performed miracles around parties, and food and suppers. His first miracle was at a wedding. Weddings are the celebration of a marriage and the joining of two families together. It means breaking bread together and celebrating the union of two individuals and two families. Future generations will be shared by both families when grandkids come along. Jesus performed the miracles of the loaves and fishes, so that the people could eat and hear the gospel preached. Jesus broke bread with his disciples. At the Last Supper, He even broke bread with the man who was to betray Him. Jesus seems to have loved a picnic and loved to sit at the table. *(Luke 22:14)* Jesus had breakfast *(John 1:12)* with His disciples after He was resurrected. Jesus loved to fellowship at mealtime! It was at the Last Supper that John the Beloved laid his head on the Master's chest.

Mealtime in our family was a time of coming together, a time of sharing our day one another. It was for us, as parents, a time to celebrate daily the fact that we saw the rich blessings of God, "your children like olive plants around your table." We always had a family dinner. My husband is an Italian and they didn't just eat in his family, they tarried for long periods of time at the table. Great memories were built around the Campo family table. We made family dinner a priority. Even when there were just two of us, I made dinner and we sat at our small table and shared our day. When our children came along we had dinner together, even if one of us was in a high chair! As our children grew in number and age, we still valued our time at the table.

When our firstborn son was in college he wrote a paper about the trials and tribulations of being subject to having dinner together every night. I cherish his words to this day:

"My parents gave me an ample amount of freedom with my friends growing up. There were very few things they demanded of me, but one thing they would not tolerate from us, was that we miss dinner. It was simply not allowed. They used to tell me it was family time and we needed to be together. Somehow it never really clicked with me. After all, none of my friends had it so rough. Some of them didn't have to be home at any special time, they ate when they got hungry! What really bugged me was the fact that what took their families only 15 minutes, took my family at least an hour. I could not figure out my parent's obsession with family time.

"I'm 21 now and I've come to realize what made that time so special for my parents: it was chemistry. If three of the five kids were there, something was incomplete and, if four were there, there was still a noticeable missing presence. Of course, we're all different, in personalities and ideas, but there's a common denominator that links us.

"After moving to Florida at 12 years of age, I began to hear it everywhere, 'I live with my mom.' 'I had a fight with my step-dad.' 'We're going to see our real dad this weekend.' Divorce, I never remember hearing much about it. I never really thought seriously about it hitting our family. If there was a place of stability in my formative years, it was my family I'm now 22 and it's time for me to start a family of my own. I'm moving out of the Campo house but, I'm not breaking up the team. There will always be a place for me at the dinner table and when I come home there will always be that same chemistry, because we are a family."

One of my son's further complaints was that "we never answered the phone and the TV was not invited to participate. It was just the family crew, and no outside interference."

This paper is one of my most cherished possessions. Now when we get together, all 22-plus of us at the same time and same place, we need several tables, but mealtime is a place of sacred memory for the Campo family! Dinner table is where we remember that we not only love each other, but genuinely like one another. We have become a fast food society and the miracles of bonding and caring for one another at the table have slowly been passed over. We have football and baseball and ballet and gymnastics. Moms and Dads run in the door grab the kids and a burger on the way. They switch kids and take off to different sports fields. Then they return home, shower, do homework and go to bed. We have created our own vicious cycle that is robbing families of getting to know one another and it repeats itself.

A recent article in *Time Magazine*, June 12, 2006 took a look at the effect of family mealtime. The article went on the say that it's at the table where a family trades ideas, confesses to one another, irons out problems, forgives one another and repairs relationships. The food may be home done or fast food, but the interaction anchors a family. When the atmosphere is right and the family stays a little longer, rather than rushing off, the gathering acts "like a kind of vaccine" protecting the members from all kinds of harm.

A survey by the National Center on Addiction and Substance Abuse at Columbia University, after a decade of date gathering, showed that family dinners get better with practice, the less often the less successful. Among families that eat together three or less times a week, 45% have the TV on and little interaction between members. Kids in those families are more than twice as likely as those who have meals together more frequently, to say there is tension among the family and they are much less likely to think their parents are proud of them.

The older our kids become the more they need safe time with family members. They also feel more secure, protected and are more open. More 12 year olds have dinner with the family 7 nights a week; fewer 17 year olds – one quarter in number-have the same 7 night meal pattern.

The survey showed that less educated parents tended to have more family meals and in the ethnic arena 50% of the Hispanic kids ate with mom/dad 6 times per week versus 39% of Caucasian teens and 40% of black teens. 40% of the kids who share family meals more, tend to get mainly A's and B's.

Anthropologist Robin Fox, from Rutgers University remarks, "If it were just about food, we would squirt it into their mouths with a tube. A meal is about civilizing children. It's about teaching them to be a member of their culture." Fox goes on to say, "Making food is a sacred event. It's absolutely central – far more central than sex. You can keep the population going by having sex once a year, but you have to eat three times a day. It's like the American Indians, they said a prayer over food. That is civilization. It is an act of politeness over food. Fast food has killed this. We have reduced eating to sitting alone and shoveling it in. There is no ceremony in it."

In addition we replace the dining table with stackable, foldable portable tables placed in front of a televisions set! Where's the trade-off? Disaster looms.

William Doherty, family and social science professor at University of Minnesota, and author of *The Intentional Family*, says, "We're talking about a contemporary style of parenting, particularly in the middle class, that is overindulgent of children. It treats them as customers who need to be pleased." Some parents offer menus – anyone eats what he/she wants, allow the children to come and go at their pleasure and even allow them to eat in the den or in their rooms. Children often do not have balanced diets – soda has replaced milk and dessert gets served whether the child eats the real meal or not. The family unit is secondary and each individual member becomes more important than the whole. It becomes an "It's all about me" syndrome. Encouraging the "I", instead of family and eliminating the concept of family as a team, leaves danger lurking in the background of ignorance and deception.

Let me strongly encourage you today, mother, to reinstate or continue family mealtimes. If you have been duped into believing, "We don't have the same schedules" or "We have too much else going on", reflect on the truth of those statements. We all have priorities. Meals together should be among them. It can become a life or death situation, your family's.

Try this for a while and you will see some worthwhile family changes. If you work and getting that dinner prepared seems impossible, plan in advance. Get the family to pitch in – a novel idea for some of you. It's about building relationships, that's how we build family. The reports have been written and the studies are in, the kids who spend time at the family dinner table are proving more successful, more fulfilled, and more solid citizens. So are their parents.

13 • MOMENTS OF MEDITATION
IN THE
MIDST OF MADNESS

They tell me I need to pray,
To visit with God every day.
Oh, for the moments to sit and meditate.
If only my husband and kids would wait!
Show me, Lord, how to blend all I need to do,
So I can spend some precious moments alone with You!

Have you ever been told get up earlier? Start you day off with the Lord before anything else. You must begin your day with the Lord – get up earlier so you'll have time. Begin the day right and it will end right. How many of us have heard these comments over and over and been feeling guilty because it wouldn't work for us? I barely got a full night's sleep, so getting up earlier never worked when my kids were little. Where can I find prayer time, when I can't find time to finish a meal? Many years ago I became convinced that I did have time. I just need a shift in my thinking and a rerouting in my prayer life. I sought the Lord as to how I could FIT it in. Rework my roadmap! Yes, God wants to spend time, quality time with us in our prayer closets. My prayer closet always had one, two or three little visitors in it! I finally came to peace with the idea that my LIFE could be turned into a time of prayer. When I stopped trying to put everyone else's rules on me, get rid of the guilt trip, and move on, I was set free to worship God in many different ways. Spending time with My God has become easier and more fruitful. Yes, there are the "closet" experiences, but the *MOMENTS OF MEDITATION* throughout my day have become more meaningful amid times of refreshing.

The following are some short thoughts that have become meditations as I ponder beautiful times and experiences. My way of looking at my life has turned my work time into a time with the Lord. My whole outlook in my kitchen, laundry room, car and supermarket has been altered. I sometimes live in the MIDST OF MADNESS called LIFE! I learned from my mother, I could turn madness into meditation, moments of distress into gratefulness. I can sulk over a broken dishwasher or rejoice in having one! Some of these are from my own life, others nuggets gleaned which I have received from friends who have raised their children and are now enjoying grand parenting. Even now as I go over them, I remember how much I love being a wife, mother, and now a grandmother. Of this I will testify; I love being who I am and I say thank You, Jesus, thank You. I am excited to tell the world that I have the best "job" in the world. I do not head up a major corporation, but I am the CMO – "Chief Mothering Officer" – I am planning, preparing and putting into motion the establishment of family. It is as old as Genesis and will be here as long as life on earth continues!

❧

1. MAKING THE MOST OF SPILT MILK

Recently we had dinner at the home of a couple with a young family. Some one knocked a glass over and the mom began apologizing profusely. It was a reflective moment when I realized the joy in spilled milk. No one had spilled milk at my table for years. How boring, I thought, my life has become! There's something to be said about empty chairs and a perfect table. Personally, I prefer filled chairs and table settings that don't match.

Lord, help me to see the pleasure in the "accidents" around my table and in my home. "Come now, I will test you with pleasure. So enjoy yourself…" *(Ecc. 2:1, NASU)* Give me the heart of a thankful child as I care for Your children.

❧

2. BETTER THAN WIMBLEDON

One day in January, 1994, I happened on a interview with Chris Everett. She has been the U.S. Open Champ 6 times; Wimbledon 3 times and had been the #1 tennis player in the world. She was being asked on how her present role of wife and mother compared to those events. She went on to state that winning Wimbledon was a high that lasted two days until you go on to St. Louis for the next tournament. Now, she continued, she had found her niche. Being a mother was joy 24 hours a day. All the worldly success cannot compare to the role of watching and participating in the unfolding of the life of your child.

Lord, let me always remember "Children are a gift of the Lord; the fruit of the womb is a reward Like arrows in the hand of one's youth. How blessed is the man who's quiver is full of them." *(Psalm 127:3-5, NASU)* Keep me mindful of the real championships in life, the title that is most meaningful is the title "MOM." Let me always look to eternal rewards.

❧

3. THE REAL THING

Once I read an article that said tellers in banks had to learn every aspect of a dollar bill. Once they knew the real article, they could easily spot the counterfeit. I can read a book on things and people. However, it's only when I create a relationship with a person – build a relationship through time and study – that I can know, really know that person.

There's always one thing in every person's heart that only God and that person know!

Lord, show me the hidden needs and wants in the life of my husband and children. Let all that is hidden be brought to light so I can minister Your love to them. *(Matthew 12:2, NASU)*

4. TIMES OF REFRESHING

I just spent a day watching our grandsons play T-ball, and visit with our precious granddaughter. She and I were making plans to get together and cook something. She is a very perceptive 7 year old. She suggested we make cookies, until I said, "No, and do you know why not?" She said, "Oh yeah, Grandpa will eat them all"! I said to her, "How about we make Jell-O"? She thought for a second and said, "Can you make Jell-O"? I was reminded that today you buy Jell-O in small containers. Time has spun so fast that we don't have time for simple Jell-O making -times of refreshing!

Lord, Show me how to make time to appreciate the small and significant things. Allow me to be refreshed in you by seeing the value of all your blessings – even the ones in a box of Jell-O. Even Jesus went to the beach, got on a boat and cooked on the beach. Jesus actually had picnics on mountains sides with thousands of friends! *(Luke 5:3- 5 & John 21:12 -15, NAS)*

5. GET OUT OF DRIVE AND PUT IT IN PARK!

My friend, Debbie, recently had surgery that put her on the sidelines a bit. Her testimony was that she had been running and running always busy and very busy. She said, "Sometimes God has to put you in park to get your attention". That really spoke to my heart. My mind is like my automobile. It gets in drive and it doesn't take time to look around or even pray – it just runs and runs! I realized there are times when I am in drive. Neutral is like a momentary pause at a traffic light. There are times when I need to shut off my motor – my brain – put it in park and just sit and wait on the Lord.

Lord, teach me to pray and listen. Teach me to "wait in silence for You only." *(Psalm 62)* In silence You can speak to my heart and quiet my mind.

6. CHILDREN LEARN BY WHAT THEY LIVE WITH!

A friend had her daughter call to ask for direction and prayer. The young woman and her husband had an adopted little girl – now 21 months old. They had been called to see if they wanted a three month old little boy. The mom was concerned that their daughter would find it hard to share the attention she alone had gotten since being placed with them. The grandmother thought for a moment and said, "Hannah has only experienced gentleness and love from you and her Dad. She doesn't know anything other than the love of the Lord showered upon her. She'll do just fine. She has learned by what she lives with!"

Lord, my child will learn of You, not by what I say, or read, or preach. It is my life and my walk that will speak of You. Teach me, instruct me. "Take My yoke upon you and Learn from Me...."! *(Matthew 12:29a, NAS)*

7. GREATEST NATIONAL TREASURE
(this bears repeating)

"When all is said and done, it is the mother, and only the mother, who is a better citizen than the soldier who fights for his country. The successful mother, the one who does her part in rearing and training aright the boys and girls who are to be the men and women of the next generations, is of far greater value to her country and occupies, if only she would realize it, the more important position than any man in it. The mother is the one supreme asset to the national life. She is more important than any successful statesman, businessman, artist or scientist."

President Franklin Roosevelt

Lord, help me to keep my focus on the bigger picture; what motherhood is ALL about. It's about a future and a plan for the next generation. It's not about the daily drudgery or work. It's about leaving a legacy of life and hope. Motherhood is about the most important position in the world. Let me embrace it.

8. BLESSEDNESS AROUND YOUR TABLE!

"How blessed is everyone who fears the LORD, Who walks in His ways. When you shall eat of the fruit of your hands, You will be happy and it will be well with you. Your wife shall be like a fruitful vine within your house, your children like olive plants around your table. Behold, for thus shall the man be blessed Who fears the LORD. The LORD bless you from Zion,

And may you see the prosperity of Jerusalem all the days of your life. Indeed, may you see your children's children. Peace be upon Israel!" *(Psalm 128 NASU)*

Lord, how I thank you for all the faces around our table. Thank You for the richness in every personality. Show me the secret places of each little heart that I might touch the needs.

9. CREATED, NOT CLONED!!!
(this bears repeating)

A friend of mine told me the "hard work" in being a mother is not the physical labor – the cleaning, cooking, and maintaining of the home. It lies in the fact that you have to be a different mother for as many children as you have. "Then God said, "Let us make man in our image according to our likeness". *(Genesis 1:26 NAS)* While siblings are often alike, they are not the same. Comparisons just create competition that may or may not be productive. Each child has a different need, personality, capability. I appreciate all the gifts around my home. I should savor the differences, see the wealth in each personality and relish the differences as jewels. How I love Variety!!!

Lord, diversify me to be what I need to be for all my children. Help me avoid comparison and value the differences. Show me each treasure as a diamond; with different facets and different shapes and different clarity. Let me be as different in understanding as You are.

ℰ↭

10. ONCE A MOTHER, ALWAYS A MOTHER

Motherhood doesn't end when your child gets a spouse. You just become twice the mother. A friend of mine once cautioned me to continue to "Know well the condition of your flock, and pay attention to your herds"! *(Proverbs 27:23.* NAS*)* My friend's very happily married daughter and her husband had fallen on tough time, unbeknownst to the family. When they were made aware of the situation, the couple was in divorce court. She told me to never stop praying for your children. Never stop being a mother. Don't be a meddler – be a prayer warrior for the family.

Lord, give me discernment to uphold and support my sons and daughters when and where they need it. Give me Your heart after them. Show me how to pray, down on my knees for those I love most in my life.

ℰ↭

11. CLEAN HANDS AND A PURE HEART

"I will give heed to the blameless way. When wilt thou come to me? I will walk within my house in the integrity of my heart". *(Psalm 101:2,* NAS*)* Do I walk with more integrity in my church and scream at my kids at home? Do I make better dishes for the pot luck supper at church and scold my kids if they stick their little fingers in the icing on the cake I made for the church members? Do I pay more attention to the needs of those outside my home than inside? I have done these things in my quest to be a better, more giving person. I repented and I try to have a purer walk in the walls of my home. I have even been deceived into thinking it was more charitable to "minister" to others outside the walls of my home. There is an old axiom that says, "Charity (love) begins at home." It's at home that love is tried and tested because it must be constant.

Lord, be as a beeping sound in my ears and heart when I show more kindness and tenderness outside my home than inside. Become a hound from heaven for me. I so want to bless my family first.

ℰ↭

12. PSALM 23

"The LORD is my shepherd; I shall not be in want. He makes me lie down in green pastures, He leads me beside quiet waters, He restores my soul. He guides me in paths of righteousness for his name's sake. Even though I walk through the valley of the shadow of death, I will fear no evil, for You are with me; Your rod and Your staff, they comfort me. You prepare a table before me in the presence of my enemies. You anoint my head with oil; my cup overflows. Surely goodness and love will follow me all the days of my life, and I will dwell in the house of the LORD forever." (NIV)

Lord, show me how You carry me; care for me. Let me know You are always here – not there – HERE for me. You give me rest in cool places, refresh me by springs of water. Your love and mercy follow me all of my days. Let me meditate on the words of this psalm. It's here just for me. When I see a snowdrift or a babbling brook, let me know You put them there so I could see them and smile.

‿

13. WISDOM!

"But if any of you lacks wisdom, let him ask God Who gives to all men generously and without reproach and it will be given". *(James 1:5 NIV)*

"Give me now wisdom and knowledge, that I may go out and come in before this people (my family) for who can rule this great people of thine.(my family)". *(2 Chronicles 1:10 NAS)*

"Behold, Thou doest desire truth in the innermost being. And in the hidden part Thou wilt make me know wisdom." *(Psalm 51,6 NAS)*

Lord, You are all wisdom. I cannot do this mothering successfully without You and Your wisdom. I need You to show me the way, Just when I think I know how to do it, the rules and the game change. Grant that I may be as Solomon and lead by Your wisdom.

‿

14. WHICH SHOE?

Many years ago, my sister, Barbara, and I were going shopping with my two sons. She is a perfectionist and does everything right and does it well. My three year old hopped in the car and she told him to fix his shoes – they were on the wrong feet. He stared at his shoes and she repeated to him, "Fix your shoes. They're on the wrong way". He still remained unmoved. Finally, annoyed she ORDERED him. Bewildered and almost crying he said, "Aunt Barbara, which shoe is on the wrong foot"?

We both, my sister and I, realized that day we need to think more like a child in our commands and orders. Sometimes they just don't get it. The KISS method still works best – Keep it Simple Sweetheart! Sometimes, we don't get it!

Lord, Give me the mind and heart of a child, pure and unadulterated. Help me, Oh, God to be upright , but let me always remember the size of my audience.

‿

15. SHEEPFOLDS!

"The Lord gives the command; the women who proclaim the good tidings are a great host. Kings of armies flee. And she who remains home shall divide the spoil. When you lie down among the sheepfolds, You are like the wings of a dove covered with silver and it's pinions with glistening gold." *(Psalm 68: 11-13 NAS)*

We women, who proclaim the good news at home, far outnumber those who proclaim it from pulpits in churches. We are a "great host". We proclaim it in our kitchens, SUVs, and on the ball field. Our very words can cause giants to flee from the lives of our families. The dictionary defines "sheepfolds" as a fenced in area for the sheep – a protected area. How I rejoice in being able to be a protected area for my family. I rejoice in folding in my sheep!

Lord, Thank you for entrusting to me Your precious children – large and small, short and tall. I want to tend Your sheep as a David. Faithful, watchful, and caring. Thank You! for Your trust.

☙

16. PERFECT AND ALL ENCOMPASSING PRAYER!

I have, for many years prayed what I call my "All Encompassing Prayer", daily for my husband and children. Psalm 91 – I put their names in –

He who dwells in the secret place of the Most High Shall abide under the shadow of the Almighty. I will say of the LORD, "He is my refuge and my fortress; My God, in Him I will trust."

Surely He shall deliver you from the snare of the fowler And from the perilous pestilence. He shall cover you with His feathers, And under His wings you shall take refuge; His truth shall be your shield and buckler. You shall not be afraid of the terror by night, Nor of the arrow that flies by day, Nor of the pestilence that walks in darkness, Nor of the destruction that lays waste at noonday. A thousand may fall at your side, and ten thousand at your right hand; But it shall not come near you. Only with your eyes shall you look, and see the reward of the wicked.

Because you have made the LORD, who is my refuge, Even the Most High, your dwelling place, No evil shall befall you, Nor shall any plague come near your dwelling; For He shall give His angels charge over you, To keep you in all your ways. In their hands they shall bear you up, Lest you dash your foot against a stone. You shall tread upon the lion and the cobra, The young lion and the serpent you shall trample underfoot. "Because he has set his love upon Me, therefore I will deliver him; will set him on high, because he has known My name. He shall call upon Me, and I will answer him; will be with him in trouble I will deliver him and honor him. With long life I will satisfy him, And show him My salvation."　　　　　　　　　　　　　　　　　　　　　　　　*(Psalm 91 NAS)*

Wherever the scripture refers to I, you, him, I say they or them. Covers each and everyone and reminds me daily that God is with them in places I am not! (example: verse 1, James dwells in the house of the Lord; no evil will come or destruction fall on Theo, etc.)

Lord, Thank You that You show me how to pray, right in your Word! You cover all the bases. Why would I try to reinvent the wheel or try a different prayer, than You have given me?

☙

17. LOVE COVERS ALL!

One day while shopping with my three year old granddaughter, she had an urgent call to go to the bathroom. I gobbled her up in my arms and settled her on my hip for a quick jaunt to the nearest rest room. Well, we almost made it! As she had a little accident on my hip, she said, "Ooogh, Grandma, I just wet you. Does that gross you out"? Her father was a youth pastor so she had picked up some of the teenagers language. I just smiled at her and said, "No, honey, that didn't gross me out at all." So

81

many "things" that happen really have humor in them, if we take the time to look.

Love covers all things and even makes me appreciate some "accidents" more than I thought I ever could have. It's actually been so many years since a small child has spilled milk on my dinner table, that I rejoice when either my husband, guest or myself spill something on a tablecloth.

Lord, I have accidents, and You never stop loving me. Let me be as gracious to those whom I serve when they fall a bit short.

∽

18. FINGERPRINTS ON THE WALL!

When my husband and I were moving from the home we had lived in for many years, we thought it would be so difficult to leave ALL the memories behind. We realized that memories are for keeping and the memories were moving too. One memory in particular is very etched in our hearts. Our youngest son always wanted to be as tall as his older two brothers. He'd jump up everytime he went through a doorway to try to hit the door jam. He finally made it! But, he kept jumping until we finally saw physical evidence; his fingerprints become a permanent part of the entry to the room. Whenever the room was painted there were strict instructions NOT to remove the fingerprints or paint over them! We didn't see dirty fingerprints, we saw a little boy who grew up to become a fine man. We couldn't take the doorway with us, but we did take the memory! Now we watch Andrew put his "fingerprints" on lives.

Lord, Thank You for all the treasured memories. Like Mary, Your mother, I "ponder these things in my heart." I am thankful for the memories of fingerprints on walls and Magic Marker on my end tables.

∽

19. RIVER RAFTING THROUGH LIFE!

While visiting family in the northeast, a place of great beauty and hills and rivers, we always marveled at the wonderful weather and green everywhere. On a visit, a day of river rafting was planned for us. Convinced I wasn't in for a "wild ride" I agreed. We had an extra tire raft filled with supplies – water, treats, sun stuff. My companions got so involved in the rafting they forgot the supply raft. I took charge of the supplies. We just indulged ourselves on the trip down the river. It was peaceful and beautiful and meandering along with the flow of the current. Not fighting it or going against it, but just smooth sailing. Much like life! As long as I was letting the river direct me, and I went with the flow, the journey was a delight. When I tried to yank and direct my raft away from the way the river was going, it became a struggle and a distraction to the beauty. Much like life!

Lord, You are my River of Life. Show me how to flow with Your direction and with Your navigating so that I can relish the beauty of it.

∽

20. ENEMY #1, FEAR!

"The LORD is my light and my salvation — whom shall I fear? The LORD is the stronghold of my life — of whom shall I be afraid? When evil men advance against me to devour my flesh, when my enemies and my foes though an army besiege me ,my heart will not fear; though war break out against me, even then will I be confident ". *(Psalm 27; 1:3* NAS)

When I fret about things, I begin to fear. When I imagine negative outcomes, I begin to fear. I must take vain imaginations under control. Mind control, the world calls it.

Lord, Help me to realize that You and only You can be God in my life. When I seek to control, direct or manipulate, I am trying to take Your place. Give me quietness in spirit that I make seek Your face and seek to dwell in Your Presence in everything I do. In You, I shall fear no evil.

✑

21. WHERE YOUR TREASURE IS!

"Lay not up for yourselves treasures upon earth, where moth and rust doth corrupt, and where thieves break through and steal: But lay up for yourselves treasures in heaven, where neither moth nor rust doth corrupt, and where thieves do not break through nor steal." *(Matthew 6:19-20* NKJV*)* When our granddaughter lost her first tooth , we sent her some tooth money. (Not tooth fairy). Prices have gone up so $1 didn't work. The following year, her brother lost his first tooth and being a wise young man he knew some tooth money would be coming from Grandma and Grandpa. His tooth fell out during school and he guarded his "treasure" until after class. However, he started to play ball after school and decided that his tooth had been safe in his mouth for 6 years so he put his "treasure" in its storehouse – his mouth. He proceeded to swallow his tooth. He got his reward anyway.

What God showed me in this was that I can't put my treasure in earthen vessels or storehouses. However, I can store treasures ahead by being a generous giver in all areas of my life. I can put my treasures in human vessels.

Lord, allow me to be a blessing to others. Help me not just to be a giver, but to be a generous giver.

✑

22. LET GO OF THE GUTTER!!

One of my daughters needed to make a decision in business and she shared her quandary with her brother. The situation demanded real trust in God. Her brother told her this story. "When I was about 11 or 12, we had to clear the gutters of the fall leaves so the flow of rain was not blocked. Dad would boost me up and I'd get on the roof. After clearing all the leaves I was ready to get down. I felt so big while I was there, but getting down seemed too big of a task. Dad kept telling me to swing my legs over and hang onto the gutter. Once I did that he said to me, "Let go, son, I'll catch you. I'm right here." Now I knew Dad was there, and I knew he would catch me, but I just couldn't let go of that gutter". In my life, there have been many situations where I need to let go and trust God, but it seemed like such a big leap. It's in those leaps that I found out just how much I could trust God, my heavenly Father.

Sometimes it's easier to hold on to the gutters in life – the bad relationships, a secure but, miserable job, anger, unforgiveness, poverty mentality. Gotta let go of the gutter!

Lord, Show me the things I am holding onto that keep me from exhibiting my faith in You, my Father. Help me to trust enough to let go.

☙

23. STUFF HAPPENS!

Stuff happens! Cars break down, keys get locked in the car when your late to pick the kids up. Dinner burns when company's coming. You run out of milk for breakfast. You have a "date" with your honey and the sitter cancels. Stuff happens. Wars break out. Planes crash into the Twin Towers and kill 2900 people. Your stock portfolio for retirement crashes! Stuff happens. Nothing or no one is completely dependable EXCEPT our God. The Bible tells us that nothing can separate us from Him. We can be separated from family, health, finances, relationships, but never from God: "Who shall separate us from the love of Christ? Shall trouble or hardship or persecution or famine or nakedness or danger or sword? As it is written: 'For your sake we face death all day long; we are considered as sheep to be slaughtered.' No, in all these things we are more than conquerors through him who loved us. For I am convinced that neither death nor life, neither angels nor demons, neither the present nor the future, nor any powers, neither height nor depth, nor anything else in all creation, will be able to separate us from the love of God that is in Christ Jesus our Lord." *(Rom 8:35-38, NIV)*

Lord, I face things all day; sometimes, all night. Ever make me mindful that there is no thing I go through without You in the midst of it. Circumstances affect me, people challenge me, situations try me, but You are always there.

☙

24. ADVERSITY OVERCOMER

I love stories about high school basketball teams that come from little towns and beat the giants from the big city to win a state championship. It reminds me of the biblical account of David and Goliath. David was the youngest brother of the sons of Jesse. While his older brothers were off at battle with the likes of Goliath, David tended the sheep. He was the baby, the butt of his brothers' sneering. "What are you doing here?" they asked him when he brought supplies. Mocking your little sisters and brothers is a pastime for some families. However, David whipped the Giant. Now who's laughing? David knew he was young and a shepherd, but he also knew that he served the God of Israel and any adversity against him was against his God.

Lord, You have made me many promises in Your Word. You never promised me I didn't have to work hard, or that I'd never face adversity. What You have told me, is that I can do all things through You, Who is my strength. I serve the God of Israel.

25. WHO CAN I TRUST?

Today, we have to be very vigilant as to who we put our children in the care of. We can even be right next to them and they can fall and get cut or bruised. One day, our daughter and I were standing on the pool steps with her 18 month old right between us. In a second he slipped and was under the water. We were right there! We realized then, as we do daily, that we MUST trust the Creator of our children to care for them.

Psalm 104 is titled in my Bible, *The One Who Cares for all His works*. Here are just a few phrases. Meditate on them, embellish on them or read the whole Psalm 104: "He established the whole earth on its foundation so that it will never totter."…"He sends forth springs in the valleys. They flow through the mountains and give drink to every beast of the field; the wild donkeys quench their thirst". Beside them the birds of the heavens dwell; they lift up their voices among the branches. He waters the mountains from His upper chambers; the earth is satisfied with the fruit of His works." *(Psalm 104:5, 10-13, NASU)*

Lord, I see Your wonder, power and greatness in this Psalm. Take me aside to see how You care for the late dinner, the lost pet, the forgotten homework There is nothing too great for You. Neither is there anything too small that You do not care about it.

26. ISTHMUS!

I just listened to a sermon from one of my favorite preachers. He was teaching about the Isthmus of Corinth. After elaborating on this great city, he remembered that as a child he was watching a show called "The Little Rascals". In the episode the teacher was asking the class if they knew what an Isthmus was. She called on Stymie, a big eyed little boy. He said, "Yes ma'am, I know what Isthmus means. Isthmus be my lucky day". Yes, Stymie, everyday is a lucky – blessed day. Some days we just don't recognize our blessings. My mother used to stop my early morning complaining, in the cold NY winters, by telling me, "You put your feet on the floor, you had your first miracle of the day already. Thank God for it!"

Lord, let me take the time to see all the beauty and abundance You have created for me. Just like I like to see the smile on the faces of my children, You rejoice in seeing the smile on my face when I behold Your beauty all around me. Make me aware of the greatness of my life and let me breath thankfulness in and out. Let me remember that You have put the color into flowers, the foam on the seas, the breezes in the air, just so I can enjoy them all.

27. THE SKY IS FALLING!

Ever feel like the world is leaning over like the Tower of Pisa?

Ever think you'll never stand upright again or live in a life that's all straightened out? Have you ever felt like Chicken Little – "The Sky is Falling?" The world may crumble and fall, but I don't have to. I serve the God, Who is my help!

If the LORD had not been my help, My soul would soon have dwelt in the abode of silence. If I should say, "My foot has slipped," Your lovingkindness, O LORD, will hold me up. When my anxious thoughts multiply within me, Your consolations delight my soul." (*Psalm 94:17–19,* NAS)

Meditate on each of these words. God says it in His Word. There are hundreds of encouraging, strengthening words in the Bible. I used to read the bible, now I ponder its words. Dwell with Him for just a moment.

Lord, What a precious Father You are. Give me the heart and mind of a minstrel when I read Your Word. Give me the eye of a gemologist – let me see the wealth, the richness, the true value in Your precious Word.

✧

28. BROKEN WING!!!

One of my greatest treasures was a gift from our son when he was about 7 or 8. He came home from school quite excited that he had a present for me. He went on to tell me he found it near the bus stop. It was a pin of a wild duck. Hand painted and rather lovely, except it had one broken wing! I put that pin on my winter coat and wore it all the time. People often commented on it, "Do you know your duck has a broken wing"? Well, of course it looked like it had a broken wing, but my standard remark was," My son gave that to me"! I saw the gift and not the imperfection. One time I had the coat in the cleaners and it came back without the duck. I was heartbroken. You see that broken duck was covered in the love of an 8 year old and that was all that counted

That's how God sees me – with all my faults and flaws and a broken wing, God doesn't see anything that isn't covered by His love for me.

Precious Father, Allow me the eyes and heart I need to not see broken wings or other things that make me love less than You do.

✧

29. YES, KATIE, YOU HAVE TO GO BACK TOMORROW!!

My five year old grand niece, Katie, was going to her first day of kindergarten. Being a sweetheart and very close to her mom, she found the events of the day very difficult. Anyone who says that putting your five year old on the schoolbus for the first time, is the beginning of Mommie's freedom, has never been a Mom! When the school bus came back at three o'clock her mom and grandmother were waiting for her. Grandma had a present for the returning student. "This treat is for you to take to school tomorrow", Grandma said. Katie thought for a minute and, with a puzzled, sort of frightened look, said, "Grandma, do you mean I HAVE to go back tomorrow?"

"Yes, Katie, tomorrow and the tomorrows forever". Life is a school and we have to keep coming back tomorrow and tomorrow! Just like Katie we need to get up and keep going. Fortunately, we go with God and we never have to travel alone.

Lord, when the wash and the worry invade my day, let me see You beside me. When the keys get lost, and the school project is remembered at eight o'clock the night before, let me know that You travel beside me. Give me the strength to face each day with a new enthusiasm, with an attitude of gratitude that You have given me another opportunity.

☙

30. GRASSHOPPER MENTALITY

"There also we saw the Nephilim (Giants and sons of Anak) and we became like grasshoppers in OUR OWN sight, and so we were (seen that way) in their sight." *(Numbers 13:33,* NAS*)* When mothering and wifing become gigantic undertakings, and we are overwhelmed by our assignments that are far beyond our energies, experiences and knowledge, we need to draw on the Lord and take on a David-beats-Goliath mentality. David didn't look at his size. He looked at God's bigness. David didn't even look at his strengths. David knew Who his God was. He told the giant, "You come to me with a sword, a spear, a javelin, but I come to you in the Name of the LORD of hosts, the God of the armies of Israel, Whom you have taunted"! *(1 Samuel 17:45,* NAS*)*

When seemingly impossible tasks beset me, I have put my trust in God and His Word. In Mark the scripture says, "All things are possible to him who believes". *(Mark 9:23,* NAS*)*

Lord, I need to build myself up in my relationship with You. Direct me and guide me every step of the way. Let me not see myself as a grasshopper, but instead, an overcomer in You. Above all else, Lord, help me to know You and not just how?

☙

31 DANIELLE, DANIELLE!

Danielle, my niece, was on vacation with her mother and her two very active children – 11 and 9. When Danielle was a little one, she was a perpetual motion machine. Into more than she was out of, her mother, would often comment, "There'll be a day, when I will see you running around like a chicken with your head off, just trying to keep up with your kids". Well, now, her mother, Barbara, was witnessing it! History was repeating itself. And Mom was enjoying it! Both the 11 and 9 year old were always into something. While on this vacation, the kids kept badgering their mom with one request after another. One question after another. Finally, in frustration, Danielle asked her mother, "Mom, when do they EVER stop asking questions?" Barbara thought for a second and said. "Obviously, they don't. You're 37 and you just asked me a question!"

Lord, thank You for all the questions and all the answers. You are my example of a patient Parent, answering all my questions, hearing all my complaints, and still hangin' in there. Teach me to do the same. Give me endurance.

87

32. LIFE IN THE DASH!

When attending the funeral of a friend's husband, I got a revelation as I looked at the other gravestones. Each identified the person and gave a birth date and a death date : "Born January 8, 1942 — Deceased November 12, 2001." Neither of those dates told you anything more about the person. What they did tell you was the "DASH" in between the dates. It's in the DASH we live our lives. What did I do in the DASH? How had I lived in the DASH? Life is lived between birth and death – in the dash. It made me ponder what the dash on my stone would represent. I will be defined in the DASH

Lord, help me to live each day as a living testimony to how I lived for You between day one and the last day.

Twice, in chapter 2 in the Gospel of Luke, it talks of Mary storing up treasures in her heart and pondering and reflecting on them:

"But Mary treasured all these things, pondering them in her heart." *(Luke 2:19, NASU)*

"His mother treasured all these things in her heart." *(Luke 2:19, NASU)*

Some of the greatest gifts I have from my family are stored in a treasure chest of memories. Should I ever have to leave my home for a disaster, I would grab my photos and my treasure chest. These are not replaceable! I often will read some of them and "ponder" over the real value they have in my life. These notes are uplifting, and I could never put a money price on any of them. To me they are priceless pieces of art.

I have solicited, from some of my friends some of their treasures to share with you. In order to respect the donors I have eliminated the names of the senders.

From sons and daughters-in-love

The engraving on the card said, "From your Daughter in Law". The note attached said it better,

I know I am not "technically" your daughter. However, that has never stopped you from treating me like one. Since the day you realized I love your son, you have been terrific. I love him dearly.

Love, J

❧

Mom,

Just a note to tell you how I appreciate and love you. We always thank God for giving us a mom with such devotion to Him. A woman who loves others and is willing to show it.

Your daughter in love

❧

Mom,

Just wanted to give you this plaque.

It reads, "It takes two good women to make one good man. One is his wife and the other is his mother"

Your daughter in love.

❧

A Mother's Day card,

To the mother of my wife.

Mom, have I told you lately that I thank you for my wife?

She is an awesome woman of God.

Your son and friend, KA

∾

Dear Mom,

Thanks so much for all your help during our recent pregnancy. We couldn't have made it without the help of our family. Someone said, "It takes a village to raise a child. That's not right. It takes a family to raise a child."

∾

Dear Mom,

I am ever so grateful to have you in my life. You are very different from my own mother, but I turn to you for Godly advice and counsel. I see you in that way. I love my mother deeply and never compare you. You are there for me in many different ways. I don't say it often, but I love you very much. It is because of you I will be getting a peaceful sleep tonight and wake refreshed. I can always count on you to be fair and objective, even though you are my husband's mom.

∾

Dear R,

Thanks for being like a mom to me. I am so happy with the way our relationship has blossomed. You are an amazing mom to your sons. Although you are not my mom, all your little "motherlies" mean a lot to me. Happy Mother's Day.

∾

From a NEW daughter in love. It's sometimes difficult to call two women "MOM" and not feel like you are betraying your birth Mom. Therefore, this note was especially meaningful, It simply said, "Mom, (how's that for a beginning)?"

∾

Mom,

I know you already know this, but I just thought I'd remind you! Thanks for stickling with me through all the junk!

Love, Me

∾

From a son who is now a pastor

Dear Mom,

Thanks so much for your thoughtful reminder that you love me. Say what you want about self esteem and it's excesses, the fact remains that a parent's affirmation of her child (or the lack thereof) has a tremendous impact on the child's overall life productivity. I thank God my parent's were always there to encourage and affirm me. That encouragement has done more for me as a minister than 20 years in a seminary could ever have done.

Much love,

∾

Dear Mom,

Thanks for your steadfast love toward Dad, me and our family. You have allowed me to experience the virtue of tenderness.

Your son

&

Dear mommie,

I hope you have the baby soon and it is a girl. I will save some of my Easter candy for you. Love,

&

Dear Mother,

I love you and Daddy. I hope Daddy doesn't kill himself on his motorcycle. Love,

&

Sons can be encouragers too!

The front of the card was of a little boy struggling to get over a fence. The note inside said,

Mom, you would help this little guy over the hurdle. Dad would say, "Get over it kid" Mom, you've had some hurdles to get over and I want you to know you're doing a great job and I am thrilled every time you get over the fence." Love, J.

&

Mommy Dearest.

Thanks for making me wear that rubber band on my two front teeth because if I didn't wear it all the church members would be calling me "Pastor Gap-Tooth" I love you.

&

Mom,

My room is a mess, but I am blessed to have you and Dad. You are the best. A.

&

Mom,

I just want to encourage you after your recent "Intense discussion" with Grandparents. The reason it was received is because you NEVER complain. It is such a Godly trait and I wish to emulate it. Love, Me

&

Mom,

You're a "good" egg. The "good" eggs make it in life and do real good at it. Makes me glad there some Grandma Burke in all of us.

&

Momsie,

Having you for a friend is one of the greatest blessings the Lord has given me, even if you're just little (ha). Love your 6'2" son

&

Honey, You always got someone to love you. You bless me everyday.

Grandma,

Happy Mother's Day. An optimist says the glass is half full. A pessimist says it's half empty. A grandma says, "I bet you'd like some cookies with that."

ᴄᴏ

Mom, I just never tell you that you are beautiful, Love,

ᴄᴏ

Notes From Sisters

"Thanks for so many things, but I especially remember you lending me your favorite green dress for a first date. It was new and it was one of the times your giving taught me to be a giver and a lover."

ᴄᴏ

You never joined us in Irish step dancing because you always got your left and right mixed up. But, you have taught me that life is a dance and when it gets mixed up you can "unmix" it with God's help.

ᴄᴏ

I always remember trying to teach you to ice skate. You never did learn. But, as I wish you a happy birthday, I want to tell you how much your life has taught me to skate around the ruts and that I can always get up from a rut!

ᴄᴏ

Gifts Without Price

A visit to Ireland to Mom's homestead with my sisters and husbands, and daughter. Priceless.

ᴄᴏ

A Waterford crystal cottage from my brother in law

ᴄᴏ

My kids bringing me flowers from school for several days and finding out they "lifted" them from the nearby cemetery.

ᴄᴏ

All the Valentine and Mother's Days presents of THEIR favorite kind of chocolate.

ᴄᴏ

The COLLECTION of stick figure art work that graced my refrigerator. Now it's painting free and I miss it.

ᴄᴏ

My favorite pin – a wild duck with a broken wing.

ᴄᴏ

Favorite Mother's Day gift. One of my grandsons proudly announced that he had purchased a gift for his mother and I to share because it was all the money he had. A pair of earrings. We each got one!

❧

A pottery coffee mug that says "Lefty".

❧

The framed "art work" in my laundry room Each piece is from an unknown artist, but probably those who hold my heart and attention more because they are mine and NOT famous.

❧

The note in my car, "I, Theo, killde (killded) a hole bunch of ants in this car".

❧

A needlepoint made by our son and his wife, Missy that says, "Families are Forever."

❧

I have in my heart countless treasures that I ponder on and store them in my remembrance for my lifetime. These can never be taken from me and I am eternally grateful. These treasures can never rust away.

EPILOGUE

I believe in the Trinity, Father, Son and Holy Ghost (Spirit), One God, three persons; each with special roles in the Godhead. This is easier to understand if, I put it in a human or natural way. I am a wife, mother and grandmother. I am one person, with different positions, performances, and roles in one body. You cannot separate Joni the wife, from Joni the mother, from Joni the grandmother. However, I do different things in each role.

Likewise the Father, Son, and Holy Spirit have roles. The Father sent the Son and the Son asked the Father to send the Holy Spirit, in the name of the Son. John 14:25–26: "These things I have spoken to you while abiding with you. But the Helper, the Holy Spirit, whom the Father will send in My name, He will teach you all things, and bring to your remembrance all that I said to you". (NASU) Jesus sent the Holy Spirit to lead us and guide us and bring to our remembrance ALL that Jesus had taught us.

John 14:16-18: "I will ask the Father, and He will give you another Helper, that He may be with you forever; that is the Spirit of truth, whom the world cannot receive, because it does not see Him or know Him, but you know Him because He abides with you and will be in you". (NASU)

Jesus said, John 14:12–13, "Truly, truly, I say to you, he who believes in Me, the works that I do, he will do also; and greater works than these he will do; because I go to the Father". (NASU)

We have abiding in us the Holy Spirit and His power.

""I will not leave you as orphans; I will come to you. After a little while the world will no longer see Me, but you will see Me; because I live, you will live also. In that day you will know that I am in My Father and you in Me and I in you". *(John 14:18–20, NASU)*

The Holy Spirit is our friend. He is within us to teach us to be successful and victorious Christians. There is nothing to fear from the Holy Ghost. I attended a basketball game at a Christian elementary school and overheard two little boys, maybe 9 or 10, talking about their bible teaching that week. One kid said, "Yeah, we learned about the Father, Son and Holy Spirit this week. The Father seems like a grandpa, with a long white beard and stuff. Jesus, the Son is cool. Jesus just said the words and the earth and everything in it was made. But the Holy Ghost, man, He's the scary One!" Interestingly, many Christians in church today think the same thing. Maybe it's because some Charismatics act like charismaniacs. The real Holy Spirit is a well kept secret today. We have not come to know the Holy Spirit as comforter, friend, and helper, the Giver of all power.

The Bible talks about the fruit of and from the Spirit *(Gal. 5:22–24)*:

"But the fruit of the Spirit is love, joy, peace, patience, kindness, goodness, faithfulness, gentleness, self-control; against such things there is no law"(NASU).

95

Let me ask if you need all of these gifts to be operating in your life as wife, mother and grandmother? I need all of them, not just one of them. Truthfully, I believe we need to be "fruitcakes" to be successful in our Pulpits.

The world offers challenges no mere human being can be totally victorious over without supernatural help.

Then there are the gifts of the Spirit *(1 Corinthians 12:8-10)*, "For to one is given the word of wisdom through the Spirit, and to another the word of knowledge according to the same Spirit; to another faith by the same Spirit, and to another gifts of healing by the one Spirit, and to another the effecting of miracles, and to another prophecy, and to another the distinguishing of spirits, to another various kinds of tongues, and to another the interpretation of tongues." (NASU).

People are afraid of the Holy Spirit because they fear tongues, fear being cuckoo, fear being out of control, making fools of themselves. As I read this above portion of scripture, I first read a "word of wisdom". What mother doesn't need words of wisdom every day? Words of knowledge, second on the list. We are continually involved in situations where we aren't sure which way to go or what to decide for our little flocks. I need faith ALL the time in my Pulpit. I need faith to put my kids on the school bus, or let them go on a field trip. I need faith to let them go to a movie or sleep over night at a friend's house. I need faith when I am called on to sit up with a sick child, or put some salve on a bad sunburn, healing in my hands and my heart. I have prayed for miracles for my flock.

One year one of my girls was waiting desperately for the return of her IRS refund. Well, we prayed and I asked God to take that check out of wherever it was in the system and put it in our mailbox. Miracle of miracles, it WAS there the next day. Out of my mouth can come uplifting words, speaking good things into the lives of my pulpit hearers. Prophesy good things. Be encouraging.

As for discerning, I need to be a discerning participant in the lives of my family. I may have a caution about a decision they make. We may need to pray with one of our kids about a friend, a job or a college or a marriage partner. We don't need to be "know-it-all's" but, we can ask God to show them the whole situation. We can ask Him to bring all the hidden things into the light. "But there is nothing covered up that will not be revealed, and hidden that will not be known". *(Luke 12:2, NASU)* "Therefore do not fear them, for there is nothing concealed that will not be revealed, or hidden that will not be known". *(Matt 10:26, NASU)*

Wife, mother, grandmother, pray for revelation of the truth in the lives of your family. Revelation can be a lifesaver. Truth revealed can be an ounce of prevention and a pound of cure.

Finally, FIVE FOLD MINISTRY: "And He gave some as apostles, and some as prophets, and some as evangelists, and some as pastors and teachers, for the equipping of the saints for the work of service, to the building up of the body of Christ; until we all attain to the unity of the faith, and of the knowledge of the Son of God, to a mature man, to the measure of the stature which belongs to the fullness of Christ. As a result, we are no longer to be children, tossed here and there by waves and carried about by every wind of doctrine, by the trickery of men, by craftiness in deceitful scheming; but speaking the truth in love, we are to grow up in all aspects into Him who is the head, even Christ." *(Eph 4:11–15, NASU)*

No preacher in a church, missionary on the field, teacher in a classroom, has a more consuming ministry than the one who stands daily, long and constant than the woman with her PULPIT IN THE KITCHEN! We have just have never thought of it in this way

In my household Pulpit, I am called to train up the future "Pulpiteers". I evangelize; bring the Word of salvation and truth. As a homemaker, I pastor a small flock. Everything I do is a lesson in kindness, wisdom, servant hood, compassion

I am daily a teacher. Do I walk my talk? When I fail do I dust off my feet and try again? I preach by the way I live. Do I live in faith, or give up and succumb to fear? Children learn what they live with. What is your flock living with and what are they being taught?

And, finally, why do we need to do and develop all these fruits and gifts and five fold ministry. If we carry on the roles of wife, mother and grandma properly it is for the purpose of "Equipping the saints for the work of ministry." Building up the saints and preparing them for life.

The most important legacy we can leave our children is not jewelry, cars, houses or investments. They are able to turn into rust and have the moth devour them. Our children will grow up, and not stay children. They will deal with everything we have dealt with. They will, like David, walk among the giants on the earth. We have opportunities to equip them. We would not give our five year old the keys to the car and say, "Go." We'd help him grow up and train him/her. We wouldn't send anyone scuba diving without the proper gear. Neither would we let them watch wrong TV or movies or send them into a crack house. Nor would (or should) we allow children unauthorized access to the computer and the world on the internet. It's not invading their privacy; it's wisdom.

Along the way I have made many mistakes and many errors in judgment. I usually thought my heart was right, but then I acted out of emotion instead of faith and waiting for God to show me that my actions would have reactions. Sometimes I'd "leave my head at the door."

The most important legacy we can leave our children is a strong faith in the Father, Son and Holy Ghost. He will never leave them or forsake them. He Is God Almighty. From your Pulpit in the Kitchen weave a legacy into their lives. When we give them wings, we need only to be excited about where their wings will take them. ❧

AN INVITATION

If you have not met the Lord Jesus Christ as your personal Lord and Savior, I invite you to ask Him into your life by praying in this manner: *"Father, I acknowledge to You that I am a sinner. I have been redeemed by the Blood of Your Son, Jesus Christ. I repent of my sins and ask Jesus into my heart to be my personal Lord and Savior. I accept that He died for my sins and was raised from the dead that I might have everlasting life and reign with the Father, Son and Holy Spirit for all eternity. Amen."*

If you just prayed this prayer and truly meant it, then immediately pick up the phone and call a Christian friend and share your experience with them. Then get your Bible or purchase one and start by reading the Gospels, Psalms, and Proverbs. You're off to the most exciting ride of your life: the journey to everlasting life. *Joni*

ABOUT THE AUTHOR

Joni Campo was born in Glen Cove, Long Island, New York of Irish-American parents. It was in high school that she met her future husband, Ted. The Campos have been married 45 years, have five adult married children and twelve wonderful grandchildren. Ted and Joni have ministered on marriage and family life extensively. Together they teach Biblical principles involving the transfer of wealth and God's plan for total prosperity in all areas of the life of the believer.

It has been Joni's passion to bring instructive words of encouragement to women, wives and mothers through the Word of God and from her own mother's heart.

Ted and Joni attend Treasure Coast Victory Center in Ft. Pierce, Florida where they serve at the pleasure of God.

TO ORDER ADDITIONAL COPIES

COPY THIS PAGE — DON'T TEAR IT OUT

The Lighthousenet Publishing Company
3275 S.E. Federal Highway
Stuart, FL 34997

Internet Orders: www.pulpitinmykitchen.com
FAX Orders: 1 (772) 283-9938 with this form completed

Ordered by: _____

Address: _____

City: _____ State: _____ ZIP: _____

Day Telephone: _____ Fax: _____

Email address: _____

Ship-to (if different): _____

Address: _____

City: _____ State: _____ ZIP: _____

_____copies of **Pulpit in My Kitchen** @ $12.99 each . . . . .$ _____

Shipping: US $2.95 for 1st book and $2.00 for ea. additional _____

*****Sales tax***** Please add 6.5% for Florida addresses _____

TOTAL including shipping and sales tax (if required). . .$_____

Method of payment: ❏ Visa   ❏ MC   ❏ Discover   ❏ Check

Card number: _____

3-digit Security Code from reverse side of card: _____

Expiration date: _____

Name on credit card _____

Billing address of credit card if different from person placing order:

_____

_____

Visit our website for free information on conferences, speaking
engagements, and other related products: *www.pulpitinmykitchen.com*